The Hidden Leader

This book is dedicated to Virginia Tucker for her lifetime of love, support, and confidence.

The Hidden Leader

Leadership Lessons on the Potential Within

Dale L. Brubaker • Larry D. Coble
Foreword by Terrence Deal

CORWIN PRESS
A Sage Publications Company
Thousand Oaks, California

For information:

Corwin Press
A Sage Publications Company
2455 Teller Road
Thousand Oaks, California 91320
www.corwinpress.com

Sage Publications Ltd
1 Oliver's Yard
55 City Road
London EC1Y 1SP
United Kingdom

Sage Publications India Pvt. Ltd.
B-42, Panchsheel Enclave
Post Box 4109
New Delhi 110 017 India

Printed in the United States of America

Library of Congress Cataloging-in-Publication Data

Brubaker, Dale L.
The hidden leader : leadership lessons on the potential within / by Dale L. Brubaker and Larry D. Coble.
       p. cm.
Includes bibliographical references and index.
ISBN 1-4129-0499-4 (hardcover) — ISBN 1-4129-0500-1 (pbk.)
   1. Leadership—Psychological aspects. I. Coble, Larry D. II. Title.
BF637.L4B78 2005
158'.4—dc22   2004015950

This book is printed on acid-free paper.

05   06   07   08   09   10   9   8   7   6   5   4   3   2   1

Acquisitions Editor:	Kylee Liegl
Editorial Assistant:	Jaime Cuvier
Production Editor:	Kristen Gibson
Copy Editor:	Sally Scott
Typesetter:	C&M Digitals (P) Ltd.
Indexer:	Sheila Bodell
Proofreader:	Dennis Webb
Cover Designer:	Anthony Paular

Contents

Foreword by Terrence Deal   vii

Preface   ix

Acknowledgments   xi

About the Authors   xiii

Introduction   xv

Part I: Prelude to Leadership   1

1. The Power of Vision   3
2. The Power of Identifying and Using Your Talents   21
3. The Power of Learning   39
4. The Power of Competence   55
5. The Power of Wanting to Be There   75
6. The Power of Passion   89

Part II: The Leadership Journey   101

7. The Power of Hope   103
8. The Power of Keeping the Fire   115
9. The Power of Determination   135
10. The Power of Gratitude   147
11. The Power of Private Victories   159
12. The Power of Your Moral Compass   173
13. The Power of Coaching and Mentoring   191

Appendix   205

Notes   215

References   217

Index   219

Foreword

If you are on the firing line as a leader in your organization, you don't need any reminders that it's tough. It doesn't matter what kind of organization you are leading. You may be leading a for-profit, not-for-profit, or educational organization, but when it comes to spelling out what needs to be done, nearly everyone points in a different direction.

There is no shortage of experts who can tell leaders what to do. Their answers are clear, but, because the problems are murky, expert advice often fails to pan out. L. Frank Baum got it right when he wrote *The Wizard of Oz*. The characters were all looking to the wizard for answers to their problems. As it turns out, the wizard was not what he was made out to be. But then, he dispensed some good common sense: look inside yourself, rather than seeking outside for answers to life's dilemmas.

Without consciously realizing it, Brubaker and Coble are echoing Baum's timeless secrets of success. Leadership lessons are best forged on the firing line by mining one's personal experience. What to do next is found in the successes and failures of yesterday and today. Power comes from believing in yourself, knowing the right thing to do, and having the courage to push ahead. It's never easy and it's not always rewarding. But that's the enduring challenge of leadership. When the hope of the future is up for grabs, the stakes are very high. Brubaker and Coble provide some sound wisdom that points leaders in the right direction.

Terrence Deal,
University of Southern California

Preface

I n this book, we have tried to create a conversation with the reader that will enhance conditions for that person as learner to take responsibility for his or her own development through an inner journey by way of reflection, activities, and exercises. In particular, this book is a response to those participants in our leadership seminars who are on the firing line and want practical ideas for their leadership. We have taken each concept and attempted to make it come alive for the practicing leader as perpetual learner.

Figure 1:
LESSONS IN LEADERSHIP

The Power Within You

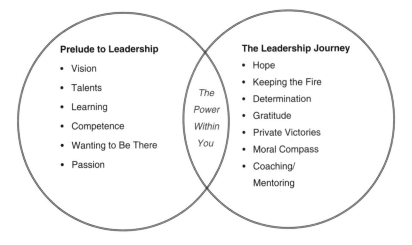

Prelude to Leadership

- Vision
- Talents
- Learning
- Competence
- Wanting to Be There
- Passion

The Power Within You

The Leadership Journey

- Hope
- Keeping the Fire
- Determination
- Gratitude
- Private Victories
- Moral Compass
- Coaching/ Mentoring

Part I, "Prelude to Leadership," contains preliminary chapters that set the stage for Part II, "The Leadership Journey." The subjects of chapters in Part I include the leader's ability to envision, recognize the value of many and different talents, learn individually and with others, see and value competence in self and others, and want to be there and have passion for realizing the vision.

In Part II, "The Leadership Journey," we discuss the leader's ability to be hopeful, keep the fire, have determination as well as gratitude, value private victories, follow a moral compass, and have the power to coach and mentor.

A variety of instructional and learning materials and methodologies are apparent in each section of the book. These materials and methodologies may be used in two primary ways: (1) as a personal guide to the reader, and (2) as an instructional tool in leading seminars or the like. A suggested readings section is at the end of each chapter. These readings will provide meaning for the reader's score on the end-of-chapter survey questions and identify possible next steps to any below-average item responses. The writing style throughout is intentionally conversational, as if we were talking directly to you and others.

The interactive nature of this resource book is reinforced by an invitation to you: please e-mail one or both of us with any questions and comments. Our e-mail addresses are given below:

—*Dale Brubaker: dlbrubak@uncg.edu*
—*Larry D. Coble: lcoble@schoolleadershipservices.com*

Acknowledgments

We wish to express our appreciation to the many people who helped us shape and refine this book. Leadership seminar participants were actively involved in reading parts of the book, and they also provided feedback as they participated in the activities that are in each chapter.

In particular, we want to thank Linda Burgee, R. Daniel Cunningham, and Paul Strickler for suggesting the title and subtitle of the book. They were in a seminar breakout group that did the first drawing of Figure 1—the figure that illustrates the organizational outline of this book.

Finally, we express our gratitude to Kay Meekins, editor of *Bizlife* (formerly *Business Life*), the magazine that originally published the preliminary essay in each chapter of *The Hidden Leader: Leadership Lessons on the Potential Within*.

Corwin Press gratefully acknowledges the contributions of the following reviewers:

Ruth C. Ash
Dean, School of Education & Professional Studies
Samford University
Birmingham, AL

David C. Munson
Principal
Meadowlark Elementary School
Billings, MT

Carole Biskar
Principal
Tualatin Elementary School
Tualatin, OR

William D. Silky
Professor of Educational Administration
SUNY Oswego
Oswego, NY

Dr. Joanne Monroe
Director of Curriculum & Instruction
Clinton Township School District
Annandale, NJ

Susan Stewart
Curriculum Coordinator
Jackson Local High School
Massillon, OH

About the Authors

Dale L. Brubaker is Professor of Education at the University of North Carolina at Greensboro. He has also served on the faculties of the University of California, Santa Barbara, and the University of Wisconsin, Milwaukee. He received his doctorate in foundations of education from Michigan State University. He is the author or coauthor of numerous books on education and educational leadership, including *Creative Curriculum Leadership* (Corwin, 1994, 2004), *Staying on Track: An Educational Leader's Guide to Preventing Derailment and Ensuring Personal and Organizational Success* (Corwin, 1997; co-authored with Larry D. Coble), and *Creative Survival in Educational Bureaucracies.*

Larry D. Coble is Managing Associate with School Leadership Services, a division of The Coble Professional Group, a leadership and management consulting organization, and Director of the Collegium for the Advancement of Schools at the University of North Carolina at Greensboro. He provides speeches and seminars on leadership nationwide. He was a Senior Program Associate at the Center for Creative Leadership and served as assistant principal, principal, and superintendent in school systems in North Carolina. His most recent superintendency was in Winston-Salem, North Carolina. He received his doctorate in educational administration from the University of North Carolina at Greensboro. He is coauthor of *Staying on Track* (Corwin, 1997; co-authored with Dale L. Brubaker).

Introduction

"Light the Fire Within"

XIX Winter Olympics 2002

This book is based on a number of assumptions that we wish to share with you, the reader. First, each of us has the ability to lead if we exercise the power within us. To deny one's power to make a difference is to participate in a kind of pseudo innocence, an almost childish "common defense against admitting or confronting one's own power."[1] In his book titled *Power and Innocence*, Rollo May refers to playwright Arthur Miller's statement that "the perfection of innocence, indeed, is madness."[2] Our second assumption focuses on our definition of power: "Power is the ability to make something happen or to keep it from happening."[3]

To say that each of us has the ability to exercise power through something called leadership is not to say that the talents we bring to this process are identical. Our third assumption is that each of us can profit from leadership lessons learned, just as we have learned from a variety of life-experiences. Perhaps Morgan McCall says it best: "Whatever the gifts that start the journey, the events and experiences that unfold along the way will shape where a person eventually ends up."[4]

Our fourth assumption follows from the third. Creative leaders are challenged to help others identify and use their talents in learning settings. These learning settings have their own personalities in much the same way that individuals have personalities. The creative leader asks, "How can I get persons with talents into experiences that will help them grow in order to benefit others as well as themselves?" To simply drop persons into difficult learning experiences is to risk their losing confidence. They must, instead, be introduced into a learning setting at a speed that will help them learn while at the same time they have enough confidence to succeed. The model for this was Coach Bill Walsh's slow introduction of quarterback Joe Montana into the San Francisco 49ers' system.

A fifth assumption with regard to leadership lessons is that "because it can be disruptive, expensive, risky, and politically difficult to move people to different experiences, it is important to consider mechanisms for moving experiences to people who need them."[5] The major point of all of this is that leaders in learning communities recognize that persons learn best by facing meaningful new challenges. And persons and organizations must recognize that anxiety will always accompany the creative process, whereby potential becomes actuality.

Our sixth and final assumption is captured in the subtitle of our book, "Leadership Lessons on the Potential Within," and the quote from the 2002 Winter Olympics at the beginning of this introduction, "Light the Fire Within." Not only must we realize that we have within us the power to make a difference, but we must light and keep the fire within us so that others can benefit from our efforts. The positive energy that we share with others largely comes from our own curiosity to learn and act on the basis of such learning. In other words, leadership lessons, when acted out, generate confidence in oneself and others. These lessons, when acted on, can keep the person and the organization on track. This leads us to the matter of sources of power.

SOURCES OF POWER

What are the sources of power available to creative leaders—those leaders who use their talents to help others identify and use their talents? **Positional Authority** is power by virtue of one's position in the organization. It is commonly associated with bureaucratic forms of organization, because those with more positional authority give "commands" to their subordinates, who have less. Regardless of the respect, or lack of it, accorded the person with positional authority, the bureaucratic subordinate is expected to obey such commands. Traditionally, it has been drawn upon heavily, but observers in the area of leadership education argue that drawing on positional authority is much like using a battery: The more you use it, the less there is to use in the future. They, therefore, recommend that positional authority should be suspended by the leader whenever possible. Morgan McCall says this best: "The trend toward moving authority down and eliminating layers of hierarchy . . . has shifted effective leadership from autocratic to empowering, with the resulting requirement that people successful with one style must shift to a new one. One might say that the territory changed underneath them."[6]

Expertise is a source of power attributed to persons because of their recognized ability to do something well. A leader may be known as a well-organized person who has demonstrated expertise in writing reports or grant proposals. She is, therefore, asked to head a team assigned this kind of work. Another leader may have special talent in speaking in formal settings. This person is, therefore, asked to speak at rituals in which the organization wants to put its best face on for the public. The secret to using the expertise of persons within an organization is that key members must be willing to publicly acknowledge and honor the talents of those expected to use them. Some leaders are reluctant to do this as they feel that honoring others will somehow diminish their own stature.

Succorance is an informal kind of power that leaves others with the feeling that they are supported emotionally. It is commonly associated with counseling and coaching. "You can do it" is the message conveyed. This is an especially important source of power when members of an organization feel they have their backs to the wall. At this point, in particular, the morale of the organization depends on this kind of support.

Charisma is a sort of magnetic charm often equated with sex appeal. Nonverbal messages, such as smiles and nods of approval, are the vehicles of communication used by the charismatic leader. Style of dress and the leader's bearing give added charisma. At the base of the charismatic leader's power is energy—energy that moves those under its influence.

We point out to seminar participants that the transformative leader integrates the sources of power in a manner appropriate for a particular situation. This integration is the kind of artistry used by a symphony's conductor—a person who is not an expert on each of the instruments but has the special talent to know when and how to draw on the talents of members of the orchestra. The term used to demonstrate this position of eminence is *Maestro*. Stated another way, fixed-template models of effective leadership miss the mark. They ignore the reality of changing contexts and times.

The initial question asked by the seminar participant—"How can I judiciously use sources of power available to me in order to accomplish my goals and objectives *and* the goals and objectives of my organization?"—has a personal face and an organizational face. *My goals and objectives* are the personal faces, whereas *the goals and objectives of my organization* are the organizational face. Returning to the *Staying On Track* metaphor, the individual wants to stay on track and so does the organization. Advice from a sage would be to *know thyself and know thy organization*. Hopefully, most of the time there will be little dissonance between the creative leader's goals and objectives and the creative organization's goals and objectives. When there is such dissonance, the creative leader must have the skills and knowledge to reconcile contradictions, if possible. Much of the writing in this book speaks to this challenge.

THE IMPORTANCE OF CONTEXT

American culture and history demonstrate a strong bias in favor of the individual. We have been taught that it is the dramatic action of the individual that makes a difference. The hitting of a home run serves as an example. When we think of psychology, we think of the psychology of the individual. In fact, however, the psychology of the collective, the group, the setting, and the community is certainly of equal importance. It is the set of circumstances that surround individual actions, the *context*, that helps us find meaning or explanation for the particular actions we participate in and observe. It must quickly be added that we are part of contexts already created, while at the same time we are in the process of creating new contexts. This makes the point that there is always a struggle between stability and change. There is also within each of us, according to psychiatrist Arnold A. Hutschnecker, "a constant battle between the forces of excitation and inhibition."[7] Recognizing this can be helpful in being kind to ourselves as well as others as we create learning settings. There can be a difference in doing unto others and doing with others.

Creative leaders know that individuals must find predictability in organizational contexts in order to gain the security needed to do good work. It is for this reason that covenants or relationships with persons are initiated and maintained. These covenants vary with respect to *intensity* and *duration*.

Covenant 1: Little Intensity and Brief Duration

Our technologically advanced society encourages many covenants that are pleasant but taken lightly. They also don't last very long. The seasoned airplane passenger experiences this kind of covenant. Flight attendants and others are pleasant and, in fact, frequently act as if they are creating another home setting for the customer. If you recognized a flight attendant in a department store later in the day, however, you probably wouldn't go out of your way to say hello in spite of congenial rhetoric earlier in the day.

Many of the civilities observed in organizations are also of this nature. Entrance and exit rituals serve a similar function. We want to feel invited into a new context and we also want to leave that context with a good feeling after doing business. The technical dimensions of doing our business may be described as the "bricks" that create structure for our relationships, but the "mortar" that holds the bricks in place is the civilities, those small behaviors that facilitate an exchange of information and feelings.

Covenant 2: High Intensity and Brief Duration

This relationship exists when a police officer gives you a ticket or you are "called on the carpet" by a bureaucratic superior. The negative spirit of this encounter makes it a perfect fit with top-down, bureaucratic organizational structure. There is no pretense with these structured contexts that this is community building. A positive spirit exists in this kind of covenant when a speaker inspires you during an hour-long presentation. If there is a promise of community by the speaker or host, this is, in effect, a kind of pseudo-community. Another example of positive spirit created by a bureaucratic superior is when you are publicly honored for something you have done. The brief duration of this event tends to erode the "high" you have felt as you settle into the rhythm of your daily tasks.

Covenant 3: Little Intensity but Long-Term

We participate in some committees whose meetings illustrate this kind of covenant. They meet at a certain time each week or month and little is accomplished. Their ritualistic nature was aptly described by one committee member: "I only hope that I die during one of these committee meetings because the distinction between life and death will be so subtle." Some people within organizations enjoy attending these meetings because they fill the time of day and keep them from having to do some of the hard work of the organization. These same people often find the socializing at such meetings a way to maintain their affinity with colleagues.

Covenant 4: Intense and Long-Term

This is the rarest kind of covenant because of the human and non-human resources demanded. Ownership by parties to the covenant is obvious in the seriousness and humor exhibited by persons who enter into true community. Persons of opposing views share a mutuality of purpose in spite of their differences, and they care enough about each other and the community to truly listen to each other. Many and diverse talents are publicly identified and celebrated.

Throughout this book, we will give attention to contexts in which power is exercised and the kinds of covenants initiated and maintained in order to achieve personal and organizational goals and objectives. It should be obvious that creative leaders will be expected to participate in the four kinds of covenants discussed in this introduction. Having this four-part framework in mind should be helpful to the leader in two ways: (1) as an assessment tool so that the leader knows what kinds of covenants are already in place in an organization and can wisely allocate resources in order to play the leader-roles expected; and (2) as a planning tool so that covenants consistent with the leader's priorities can be created. The next section of this introduction has been written with this in mind.

LEARNING SETTINGS AS CONTEXTS

Given the importance of creating learning settings, we were surprised to discover that "ability to learn . . . has not been mainstream in the research on leaders."[8] A major reason for this is that "in an achievement-driven context, people are inclined to focus on performance rather than on growth."[9] The politicizing of organizational cultures is illustrated in the following story about the superintendent of a large school system who called together his central office staff and said the following:

> We need to identify those schools with low test scores, after which we will do what needs to be done to bring about an incremental positive change in the scores. Because you, as curriculum leaders, are in charge of the curriculum and the testing program, I will hold you account-able for raising the test scores. I will give you the funds to raise the scores. If you are successful, there will be plenty of money for you to attend conferences of your choice; if you are not, you will stay at home. Higher test scores will make us appear to be winners. I want to be a winner.

Leadership seminar participants have shared with us similar stories from their own business and governmental settings. For purposes of our discussion, it is simply important to note that our emphasis on creating learning communities is, at times, an upstream effort that depends on our wise and judicious use of power—the theme and thesis of this book. These efforts must be directed at a key question: "What can go right and wrong as learning communities are created and why?" One hallmark of the leader who creates and maintains learning communities is the ability to describe what has been done, what is being done, what should be done, and what can be done in a democratic, ethical framework. In valuing the creation of learning communities, attention must be given to both opportunity and responsibility, two forces that sometimes seem at odds with each other in our society. As discussed briefly in this section of the introduction, today's leaders face a fundamental tension in trying to reconcile accountability measures that can promote standardization with developmental needs and interests of organizational personnel and those they serve.

CONCLUSION

Our aim in this introduction has been to involve you in the challenging and exciting process of creating learning settings that will release the talents of all involved in such communities. The benefits of this are many: the creative leader's ego will be kept in check due to the importance of the learning process rather than having self-gratification as the primary norm; activities will have meaning rather than simply being mindless activity; and participation in community can combat loneliness and isolation often felt by people who are simply going through the moves at work. We now move to how the creative leader can set the stage so that all persons involved can use *the power within to stay on track.*

Part I

Prelude to Leadership

1

The Power of Vision

Dale L. Brubaker

I n order to truly understand how a leader's vision can be an important source of power, we have to go back to the basics—the dictionary's definition of the term. Vision is the act or power of anticipating that which will or may come to be. Noted journalist and historian David Halberstam, writing in his best-selling book titled *War in a Time of Peace,* applauds Colin Powell for a refined sense of anticipation throughout his career. It is this sense of anticipation that Powell used in order to help his bureaucratic superiors understand what was coming down the pike.

Powell was not an honor student in high school, and it was only when he joined ROTC at City College of New York, from which he graduated in 1958, that he discovered the discipline that gave him focus and meaning. A child of Jamaican immigrants who worked in New York City's Garment District, Powell appreciated the fact that the army gave him clearly stated, straight signals—something that resonated with his intelligence, hard work, and drive. Powell's autobiography, *My American Journey,* sold 1.3 million copies—a tribute to readers' belief in the American Dream.

Powell's story is mirrored by many other Americans who felt empowered by "the dream"—a vision of what they could become. Lee Kinard, a former host of *The Good Morning Show,* America's longest running and most successful local television show, tells the story of how his dream for a better future served as a life-saving beacon when, as a child, he was sent to care for his alcoholic and abusive father in West Virginia. Kinard, in his best-selling book, *Good Morning,* relates how he failed the seventh, eighth, and ninth grades, after which a few caring teachers helped him turn his life around. Kinard had a small desk in the hallway of a cold, run-down, West Virginia house, and it was there that he began to discover and use his intellectual skills that ultimately led to a doctorate. It was part of his mission in life to tell his story and share his dream with school children, particularly those at risk, throughout North Carolina, Virginia, and West Virginia.

Madeline Albright's life story demonstrates the power of vision in achieving the American Dream. She was born in 1937 in Czechoslovakia, where her family suffered from the domination of the Nazis and the Communists. Entering the United States at age 11, she exercised her family's interest in foreign policy by founding foreign policy clubs in her schools. Her fluency in four languages and her writing and speaking skills stood her well when, later in her life, she became a National Security aide in the Carter administration. She later became the first female Secretary of State, during the Clinton administration.

It is interesting that, for Powell, Kinard, and Albright, it was not enough for them to simply have and fulfill their personal dreams. They also had the strength of their convictions and willingness to share such dreams, as well as their life stories, with a wider audience.

ARTICULATING THE VISION

Father Theodore Martin Hesburgh, upon retiring from the presidency of the University of Notre Dame after thirty-five years, was asked about the secret to his self-assured sense of command. He responded: "The very essence of leadership is you have to have a vision. It's got to be a vision you articulate clearly and forcefully on every occasion. *You can't blow an uncertain trumpet.*"[1]

Many of us have come to the place where we have little faith in written vision and mission statements. It is from walking around the building with a CEO, governmental leader, or a school principal—and from observing their verbal and nonverbal behavior, as well as others' reactions to them—that we learn the officially appointed leader's real vision, or lack thereof. A school principal, for example, demonstrated that she cared about her school by walking me to my car in the parking lot, all the time talking about how proud she was that the staff did everything they could to reach every child. The stories she told revealed the authenticity of her convictions.

The role that focus plays in articulating the vision of an organization was brought home to me several years ago while having breakfast with a university police officer. He told me the story of a fellow officer, whom I shall call "Bob." Bob's problem was that his original goals were often displaced by immediate concerns. "Bob would drive down an alleyway to investigate the theft of equipment from a building. He would stop his car suddenly and begin to write a ticket for an illegally parked car. His partner would remind him that the police car was blocking two cars from proceeding down the alley, and the original reason for this trip was to investigate the theft of equipment from a building."

It seemed that Bob's partner had a fulltime job in getting Bob to the right place at the right time.

Once again, a key ingredient of focus is the strength of one's convictions. William F. Buckley brought this to my attention in his book, *Atlantic High*. "Ken Galbraith and I have in common what strikes some as a disadvantage, but it isn't: namely, our plainspoken bias, which gives a harnessing energy to our work."[2] Their biases were not the same, given the fact that Galbraith is a liberal Democrat and Buckley is a conservative Republican, but, nevertheless, their convictions energized them.

I can't conclude this discussion without telling a story about vision that brought my attention to its real, night-after-night value on the North Carolina coast. For several years, a few neighbors and I took our teenage children on fall fishing trips to the Outer Banks. On one occasion, two of my children and I walked into the town of Buxton to shop at a well-known bait-and-tackle store. We became so engrossed in the store's contents that we failed to see that it was getting dark. Because it was our first visit, I became disoriented when we walked out the door. My confusion was quickly dispelled when the sweeping beam of the lighthouse engulfed us. We sure-footedly made our way to the campground next to the origin of the beam.

Likewise, your vision, or anticipation of what should and can be, will help you as a leader when you find yourself in life's many wildernesses. Hold fast to your personal and organizational dreams, for they will often bring light when you least expect it—a gift to others and yourself. Grounded in your understanding of the past, you will find meaning in the moment while, at the same time, having an eye on important new directions for the future. In short, you will be living, and thus sharing with others, the power of your vision.

Implications for Leaders

Larry D. Coble

ORIENTATION

The process of visioning falls within the realm of developing a personal vision for one's life, within the context of both an organizational identity and a personal identity. A leader can have a vision for her life outside of the organization, a vision for herself within the organization, and a vision for the organization and those she leads. Visionary leaders will choose to create visions around their personal identity at home and at work. They will certainly lead the visioning process for the organizations in which they work, whether their responsibility is for leading a department in a company, a corporate division, a hospital, a classroom, a school, a school system, or any other organization.

Many who write about the process of visioning and visionary leaders have tended to oversimplify these concepts, often suggesting that the creation of a vision and visionary leadership is a cognitive activity. In other words, one might infer that once I decide to develop a personal vision or a vision for those I lead, all that remains is to "install" the visioning process. It simply does not work that way. Visions and visionary leaders develop over time through reflection, communication, and connection with others. Based on our research, the research of other scholars in the field of leadership development, and our life experiences at work and at home, we can offer suggestions that will enhance and accelerate the readers' personal development in the area of visioning and visionary leadership.

My personal belief is that developing a vision and becoming a visionary leader will always be a work in progress. I have found that to be visionary does not mean that there is necessarily a once-and-for-all vision. As a leader, you go as far as you can see at any given time. A vision is about the future, and it does provide direction. It includes speculation, making assumptions, and making value judgments on the part of the leader. As circumstances change and values are reevaluated, visions are altered in keeping with the growth and development of the leader and the needs of the organization.

TRANSFORMATIONAL VISIONING

Powerful visions that tend to transform individuals and organizations become extremely personal. The vision is appropriate, in the mind of the leader, for himself and the organization he leads. The visioning process that leads to transformation reflects an idealism that causes others to want to get on board. The visionary leader creates conditions under which others feel inspired and committed to something greater than themselves. Visionary leaders are able to literally "paint a picture" with their words, which leave stakeholders with an understanding of purpose and direction.

Visionary leaders are skilled communicators. They are able to communicate their visions in a way that their followers feel new energy and a shared responsibility and a shared accountability. This renewal seems to be built on the idea, that by "buying in," there is hope for a future that is clearly better than the current set of circumstances.

One very powerful example of a visionary leader is Walt Disney. His vision for Disneyland was one that captured the heads, the hearts, and the hands of all those associated with his enterprising genius. Look at the picture that Walt painted with his words and see how, after reading his vision, you actually feel tremendous hope and excitement about a future that will be better for everyone:

The idea of Disneyland is a simple one. It will be a place for people to find happiness and knowledge. It will be a place for parents and children to spend pleasant times in one another's company: a place for teachers and pupils to discover greater ways of understanding and education. Here the older generation can recapture the nostalgia of days gone by, and the younger generation can savor the challenge of the future. Here will be the wonders of Nature and Man for all to see and understand. Disneyland will be based upon and dedicated to the ideals, the dreams and hard facts that have created America. And it will be uniquely equipped to dramatize these dreams and facts and send them forth as a source of courage and inspiration to all the world.

Disneyland will be something of a fair, an exhibition, a playground, a community center, a museum of living facts, and a showplace of beauty and magic. It will be filled with the accomplishments, the joys, and hopes of the world we live in. And it will remind us and show us how to make those wonders part of our own lives.[3]

My guess is that practically every individual associated with the Disney organization, once they heard Disney's well-articulated vision, could quite easily understand the concept of Disneyland. They certainly began to realize that there would be no other theme park as unique as Disneyland, and that, if they were able to make Walt's vision become a reality, they would create an organizational uniqueness that would make their park truly special.

SHARING IN THE TRANSFORMATION—
A PERSONAL APPROACH

Walt Disney articulated a powerful transforming vision that resulted in Disney theme parks throughout the world. What he did with his vision was to create a direction that enabled individuals to begin to sort out their own roles in the accomplishment of the larger super-vision. He realized that, for his vision to be accomplished, each and every Disney employee or "cast member" would need to create a personal vision that would contribute to the corporate effort. Disney recognized, as do all visionary leaders, that shared vision begins with personal vision, his own and the personal visions of all his employees.

The hope for a "better future" constructed around a theme park like no other meant that they, as Disney employees, through their individual and collective contributions, could make the vision come alive. Effective leaders, such as Walt Disney, tend to "enroll" their followers with the "corporate identity," and, as a result, followers commit and share in the pride that goes with being a part of something greater than themselves.

From my experiences in having led several large complex organizations, if the visioning process is successful, each "player" creates her own view of the larger vision. This means that each individual in the organization has a view of the future that is aligned with "the" vision but is unique at the same time. Organizations become transformed when individuals create personal visions that are aligned with the larger vision, but they carry with them the uniqueness of their individual contributions. People have a choice. When they choose to enroll in the process, attaining the vision becomes a force in their hearts and becomes intrinsically motivating. The result is an emotional commitment and not just compliance.

MAKING THE TRANSITION TO VISIONARY LEADERSHIP

Having had a long career in leading organizations, and based on my work over the last decade in leadership development, I've grown to believe becoming a visionary leader requires an effort of conscious soul searching and more. To attempt to become visionary through some cookbook approach does a severe injustice to the process of leading. Visionary leadership is more of a function of who you are becoming and not so much who you are. It does, however, require an in-depth understanding of who you are if you wish to "become" visionary.

In order to help you jump-start your journey to visionary leadership and stay on track with your leadership development, consider the following recommendations:

- Take the time to reflect on your early childhood beginnings and be honest with yourself about early childhood experiences that played a significant role in the person you are today. This reflection should include "rules" that you were taught for the purpose of running your life, as well as critical life experiences from which you learned "lessons." Recognize that this "shaping" process has resulted in the person you are today. Some aspects of this shaping help you in being effective and some aspects hinder your effectiveness. You must truly understand who you are before you can connect with others. You cannot become a visionary leader unless you are able to connect with others.
- As you begin to understand how you have been "shaped" and who you are, spend time identifying those things in your personal and organizational life about which you truly feel passionate. If you are going to become a visionary leader, it is imperative that you are passionate about the nature of your work. For example, as a hospital administrator, you may feel great passion for improving patient care; as a corporate leader, you may feel passionate about offering the best service to your customers of any organization in the industry; or, as a school administrator, you may feel passionately about providing opportunities for the economically disadvantaged students under your direction.

- Develop your skills as a highly effective communicator. Do whatever you have to do to become a master communicator. You may have the greatest vision of all time, but if you can't communicate it, then you can't lead. Take into account not only the "message," but also the way it is delivered. The words you choose should be "selling" words and should be easily understood by everyone. Go back and think about Walt Disney. You have read the written version of his vision, but imagine him and the style he used in talking about his vision. All of us can visualize his easy, confident, matter-of-fact type of delivery style, and we can visualize why Disneyland would be good for all of us.

> Consciously begin to formulate your vision. You should start by choosing key words that capture your passion and help define where you want to move the organization. Remember that you are not leading from the past, you are leading to a better future.

> Practice talking about your vision. Talk with anyone and everyone about your vision. Less is more in terms of explanation. You should say enough to capture the future direction accurately, but not so much that it is overload. Repeat your message over and over to new audiences. You will get better. Your message will improve. And your vision will become clearer with time.

CONCLUSION

The reality of leadership is that you may have gotten in touch with those aspects of your life that have contributed to your effectiveness and have addressed those that are getting in your way of becoming more effective. You may enhance your ability to communicate through a variety of methods. You may formulate your vision. You may share your vision through practice. The reality, however, is that some people will never accept your vision. Do not be discouraged. Leadership is a process, not a person. It involves the leader, the followers, and the situation. If the majority is unwilling to accept your vision, then you will need to modify it so that it is more in keeping with the culture and the times. *Majority* is the operative word here. You will probably never get 100% support, but you will need a majority in order to recognize success.

Do not compromise your dream or your passion. Recognizing when it is appropriate to modify your vision and then acting on this recognition is in itself a developmental activity. Visionary leadership also involves taking people where they are at any given time and helping them grow and develop their own ability to see a better future.

In order that you might enhance your capacity for visioning, the following exercises may prove useful. Please use them as you see fit as you evolve.

ENGAGING SELF AND OTHERS

The following activities and materials are designed to involve you, the reader, and others, as you and they create learning communities. Because our major emphasis in this book is on leadership lessons for adults, the exercises focus on adult learning.

Activity 1.1

List three major changes you believe your organization will have to face in the year 2010 and what impact each change will have on your leadership techniques, styles, or behavior.

Major Changes	Impact

Activity 1.2

We have already noted that leadership has both a personal and an organizational face. The same thing is true of vision statements. In formulating and articulating personal and organizational vision statements, your enthusiasm for things you wish to change can blind you to personal and organizational reality: in order for some things to change, other things need to be conserved. The leader who refers to himself or herself as a "change agent" intimates, with this language, that others will be expected to change without the leader being changed. The following inventories will remind you that both change and conservation are essential elements that must be recognized by creative leaders.

A Personal Change and Conservation Inventory

_____ (My Name)

What are three things about my leadership that I personally value and want to conserve?

    1. _____
    2. _____
    3. _____

What are three things about my leadership that I personally want to change?

    1. _____
    2. _____
    3. _____

An Organizational Change and Conservation Inventory

_____ (Name of Your Organization)

What are three things about my organization that I highly value and want to conserve?

    1. _____
    2. _____
    3. _____

What are three things about my organization that I want to change?

    1. _____
    2. _____
    3. _____

Activity 1.3

If your organization has a vision statement, obtain a copy of it, read it carefully, and answer the following questions:

Is the audience for the vision statement clearly stated or is the audience implicit?
❑ Stated   ❑ Implicit

In either event, do you agree that this is the appropriate audience?
❑ Yes   ❑ No

If your answer is no, please identify the audience(s) that should be addressed:

_____

Is the vocabulary level of the written statement appropriate for the audience(s) you feel should be addressed?
❑ Yes   ❑ No

Please elaborate:

_____

_____

Is the vision statement too brief, too long, or about the right length?
❑ Too brief   ❑ Too long   ❑ About the right length

Please elaborate:

_____

_____

Who were the people involved in formulating the vision statement?

_____

_____

What is the stated rationale for involving the persons cited above? *(For example, one or a limited number of persons were involved in order to write the vision statement efficiently, given time restraints. Or, a larger number were involved in order to achieve core group ownership that could then get others in the organization to buy into the vision statement.)*

_____

_____

Is the vision statement consistent with the way members of the organization talk when they walk with guests around your building(s)?

❏ Yes   ❏ No

Please elaborate:

_____

_____

_____

_____

Activity 1.4
Visionary Leadership and Changing Organizations

Significant advantages are associated with a leader who has a clear vision regarding how his or her organization should change. There may also be some disadvantages. What are some of the major advantages and possible disadvantages that come to your mind?

Major Advantages	Major Disadvantages

Activity 1.5
A Vision for Excellent Service

Can we provide it in our organizations?

Please outline a description of an experience that you remember very clearly in which you got **excellent service** in some organizational setting. It may have been in a retail store, a restaurant, a utility such as the electric or gas company, a bank, a hotel, a school, or any other organization.

Please make your notes complete enough to be able to describe the incident with details.

_____

_____

_____

Now that you have outlined the details of your experience, please answer the following questions:

Why do you remember this particular experience?

_____

_____

Were you surprised at the excellent service or did you expect it?
❏ Yes   ❏ No

Why?

_____

_____

What were your **reactions** to the good service you received, other than being pleased or flattered?

_____

_____

Do you think the good service was due to the **individual** with whom you dealt in the situation, or did it have something to do with the entire **organization** of which the individual was a part?

❑ Individual　　❑ Organization

What do you think was the **single** most important **reason** you got the good service you enjoyed?

_____

_____

In your opinion, what part did **visionary leadership** have to do with your experience?

_____

_____

Activity 1.6
Analyzing the Organizational Norms in Your Organization

Think about your organization.

List some important values, beliefs, or attitudes that are prevalent within your organization that definitely impact the behavior of your co-workers. Then review your list and place a check mark in front of those items that you feel represent the greatest obstacles to organizational change.

_____　　　_____

_____　　　_____

_____　　　_____

_____　　　_____

_____　　　_____

_____　　　_____

Activity 1.7
What Will Your Vision Look Like When it Becomes a Reality?

How will people in your organization be treated by one another?

_____

_____

_____

What will be expected from them?

_____

_____

_____

What will they be prepared to do?

_____

_____

_____

How will the people in your organization feel about going to work?

_____

_____

_____

How will people "see" your vision in action?

_____

_____

_____

_____

CASE 1: Implementing an
Assignment on Stating Organizational Vision

The head of your organization approaches you and asks you to lead a five-person committee charged with stating the vision for the organization. The four other members of the committee must now be chosen. Your first decision concerns the basis for your choices—a cross-section of the organization? a few trusted colleagues? persons with particular talents you feel are needed in order to perform tasks? individuals who have high credibility with the organizational head? persons with the most power in the organization? persons who represent the most powerful constituencies in the organization?

The second decision you consider making is what kind of orientation you will share with committee members at your initial meeting. Do you want a well-structured orientation, and, if so, of what length? Or, do you simply want to state the charge given you as chair of the committee? *What is your decision?*

After giving your orientation, a colleague says, "How seriously should we take this assignment? This may well be another fad like the other ones we have followed over the years. If so, let's simply give a minimal amount of resources to this assignment and go back to work." *How will you react to this question?* Your answer is your third decision.

The fourth decision facing you emerges from committee discussion. One member argues with some conviction as follows: "We must begin by having each member of this committee state his or her personal vision!" A second committee member counters, "We were asked to state organizational vision, not personal vision. Let's get on with it!" *What is your response?*

As your committee continues its work, it is clear that you will need a timetable. Your fifth decision is, *"What is a reasonable amount of time* that should be spent given the goals and objectives that have been agreed upon by the committee?"

_____

_____

During a recent meeting, a committee member raises the following question: "Should we involve those outside of this committee in shaping and reshaping the organizational vision statement? And, if so, how?" *What is your reaction to this question?* Your answer is the sixth important decision confronting you.

_____

_____

_____

The seventh decision is a major one: What format should the committee choose in order to articulate the vision? Should it be a conversational, simple format like that stated by Walt Disney—a more formal and sophisticated format using higher-level vocabulary? *What is your position on this matter?*

_____

_____

_____

The eighth and final decision has to do with avenues for the articulation and dissemination of the organizational vision statement. *What kinds of print and nonprint media do you wish to advocate being used? Who should be involved in verbally articulating the vision?*

_____

_____

_____

Throughout this decision-making process, you and your committee will need to decide how you will relate to the organizational head who gave you this assignment. *What guidelines will you advocate to committee members in speaking to this challenge?*

_____

_____

_____

Authors' Recommendations

The italicized questions in the previous case will help guide you through the technical dimensions of vision creation and articulation. It needs to be stated that the leader's role in these processes is very important. Members of the organization will pick up on the leader's verbal and nonverbal messages as to the importance given to vision creation and articulation. The energy level of the leader with regard to these matters will be quickly read by those expected to participate. The authenticity of the leader's involvement in vision creation and articulation is a central issue. Erving Goffman, author of the classic *The Presentation of Self In Everyday Life*, published in 1959, argues that the genuineness or authenticity of the leader is the critical element in establishing the leader's credibility. Members of today's organizations have been exposed to so many fads ("flavors of the month") that they are wary of the introduction of any new program, such as vision formulation and articulation.

SELF INVENTORY

Now that you have completed the readings and activities on "The Power of Vision," think about what you've learned and respond to the following items on a five-point scale: 1 (low) to 5 (high).

1. My ability to define vision so that others will know what it means. _____

2. My talent in anticipating what is coming down the pike in and for my organization—the organizational face of vision. _____

3. My ability to anticipate what will happen to me personally in my organization—the personal face of vision. _____

4. My ability to develop a personal vision for my life as a whole and   _____
   understand what this means for my personal identity.

5. My ability to articulate my personal vision to those with   _____
   whom I wish to communicate it and integrate my
   personal vision with organizational vision.

6. My understanding of how both personal and organizational   _____
   vision can transform the person and the organization.

7. My skill as a communicator in helping others shape   _____
   organizational vision.

8. My skill as a communicator in helping others communicate   _____
   organizational vision.

9. My ability to state organizational vision verbally, and with   _____
   conviction, in one-on-one and small group settings.

10. My ability to state organizational vision verbally, and   _____
    with conviction, in large group settings.

Note: If you are in a group setting, form discussion groups in order to share and summarize findings.

Scoring for Self Inventory
   Total the ratings and find your score in the following scale:

41–50	Superior
31–40	Above Average
21–30	Average
11–20	Below Average
0–10	Poor

SUGGESTED READINGS

Albright, M. K., with Woodward, B. (2003). *Madame Secretary.* New York: Miramax.

Kinard, L. (1997). *Good Morning.* Winston-Salem, NC: Down Home Press.

Nanus, B. (1992). *Visionary Leadership: Creating a Compelling Sense of Direction for Your Organization.* San Francisco: Jossey-Bass.

Powell, C. (1996). *My American Journey.* New York: Random House.

Scott, C. D., et al. (1993). *Organizational Vision, Values and Mission.* Nevada City, CA: Performance Learning Systems.

2

The Power of Identifying and Using Your Talents

Dale L. Brubaker

As a child, it was never clear to me whether my parents were poor or if they simply *thought* they were poor due to living through the depression and other financially threatening experiences. For example, they would drive an extra mile or so to get a dozen ears of corn ten cents cheaper than somewhere else. My father was hesitant to put more than five gallons of gas in the car because he thought having a full tank would cause him to drive more— probably to get that dozen ears of cheaper corn.

One Christmas, my brother, Bob—a year and a half older than me— and I received some gifts together . . . one desk and two chairs that my father had made himself. It was a mystery to me how he expected us to use these three items. I couldn't imagine doing my homework with my brother staring at me.

In the spring after we received the desk and two chairs, Dad returned from an out-of-town trip with a bonus gift—a new croquet set. We took it to the backyard and opened it. Our approaches to the gift couldn't have been more different. I immediately took the mallets and balls to a flat surface and started playing, *after* which I placed the wickets near where they were supposed to be.

In the meantime, Bob read the rules and drew a picture of where the wickets should go. He then figured out exactly how many hits of the ball it would take to go around the course perfectly.

During our childhood, Bob and I thought the other brother was both odd and wrong, thinking, "How could anybody think and act like that?" It was only with age and experience that we began to understand that our learning styles were very different—his left-brain orientation was linear and sequential, and my right-brain orientation more random and experiential. Perhaps even more important, each of us learned that the other's talents were needed on a team. Bob's attention to systematic thinking and details and my willingness to take risks and immediately get involved could actually support each other when given a common team goal.

THE TEAM-BUILDING PROCESS

The first step in the four-step team-building process is identifying one's own talents. A common talent inventory used in leadership seminars consists of four columns, each with a boldfaced heading: Chronology of a Best Day, My Talents Used During This Day, Sources of These Talents, Personal Decision to Continue to Use or Not Use This Talent.

In the left column, the participant is asked to record the times and activities engaged in during an ideal or "best" day. To the right of each entry are talents used during the activity, sources of these talents (i.e., parents, teachers, or coaches) and the decision whether to continue using this talent.

Participants not only discover the key role their talents play in making an activity successful, but they also appreciate important gifts from persons in previous and present generations. This is the second step in the process of team building.

The third step is to be willing to publicly acknowledge the important role that others' talents have played in your talent development. This makes it possible for you to pass the torch to others. You will be living what I have come to define as *creative leadership:* using your talents to help others identify and use their own talents. This is in stark contrast to some persons' definition of leadership as getting others to do what you want them to do whether or not they want to do it.

The fourth step in the process of team building is to publicly recognize your appreciation for other team members' talents. It's surprising how many leaders fail to take this step. Some have a teeter-totter attitude: if you go up, I go down, and vice versa. Others appear simply to be insensitive. In fact, the celebration of others' talents and successes makes you and your team look and perform better. And it has the side effect of making team members feel less lonely.

Each June, Gerald Austin, a head referee in the National Football League, receives a call from the NFL office in New York City for the assignment of his crew for the coming year. His challenge is to integrate new people and returning officials into a smoothly functioning team . . . the same task that leaders in private and public sectors face as they downsize and reorganize.

Austin has mixed feelings as he deals with the reality of the phone call. For example, he's sad about losing a 24-year veteran umpire who was both friend and roommate. At the same time, he's challenged by the prospect of training the rookie umpire.

The second member of the crew to leave is a seasoned back judge who worked the previous year's Super Bowl. He brought humor and high energy to the crew. He's being replaced by a second-year official at the beginning stage of his learning cycle.

The third official Austin loses was a rookie just two years before. While on the team, he made great progress and publicly thanks Austin for his role in training him. He's replaced by a solid 10-year veteran. The challenge is to get this veteran to do things in a way that is consistent with the culture and traditions of the crew.

Austin reminds himself that head referees, like other leaders, tend to think their way is the best way. He also communicates his belief that meaningful structure, high but realizable expectations, and patience are essential in what he calls "growing into a team."

In short, as an accomplished head NFL referee who has worked three Super Bowls, Gerald Austin uses his talents to help six other referees identify and use their talents. The result is a team of officials who make sure the game is played fairly.

Remember, there is both power and satisfaction in being a creative leader who realizes the importance of teamwork.

Implications for Leaders

Larry D. Coble

ORIENTATION

In Chapter 1, in the section titled "Making the Transition to Visionary Leadership," a reference was made to the "shaping" process and how this shaping has impacted your effectiveness as a leader. How you have been shaped plays an important part in your preference for teamwork over individual achievement, or vice versa. Shaping is the result of acquiring certain preferences that are based on what your interpretations are of early childhood experiences. In other words, you have acquired certain preferences based on a set of life experiences. At the same time, you have inherited certain preferences determined by your genetic predisposition.

You, then, are a developing leader who has been shaped by both nature and nurture. As a leader who has been shaped by both life experiences and inherited traits, you will have a natural preference for teamwork or a natural preference for individual achievement. Some of us are naturally team players; others of us prefer individual achievement to teamwork. Time after time, our work with leaders and the use of assessment instruments bear out this fact. It is extremely important to understand that it would be wrong to assume that a strong team player cannot achieve individually or to assume that a strong individual achiever cannot become a good team player. My personal experience suggests, however, that, in most organizations, there is much rhetoric about teamwork; in reality, many of our organizations are filled with individual achievers. Those leaders who tend to be highly effective seem to be the ones who can adapt their individual preferences to the current demands of their leadership challenges and who readily identify when there is a need for teamwork and when there is a need for individual achievement.

WORK GROUPS VERSUS TEAMS

A few years ago, a survey was conducted with approximately 1600 organizations for the purpose of determining employee perceptions regarding teams in their organizations. The findings were rather amazing. At significantly high percentages, survey respondents felt that the presence of teams contributed to improved employee morale, improved management morale, increased profits, improved quality of products and services, improved level of customer service, and improved overall productivity. An obvious fact is that the perception is that teams can out perform individuals.

Activity 2.1

What images come to mind when you hear the word "team"?

_____

_____

Identify the kinds of teams that exist in your organization.

_____

_____

_____

_____

Group/Team Continuum

I prefer to look at groups along a continuum, beginning with a work group at the beginning point; if the group evolves to higher levels of performance, then it can become a team. If the team continues to evolve, the possibility exists for the team to become a high-performing team. Let me be clear that your group can be a work group and be ineffective or it can be highly effective and technically not qualify as a team.

One of the more commonly accepted notions about how groups differ from teams is that, with groups, members can work independently and the group will be able to accomplish its desired outcome. One way to think about this is to assume that the work group has a good understanding of what it is trying to produce. The members of the group come together and, perhaps, the group leader makes individual assignments, the group members complete their assignments working independently of one another, and they supply the group leader with their completed individual assignment. The group leader then assembles the individual assignments into the "whole" that is needed to successfully complete the project. It is important to note that under the work group approach, members do not need to feed on the energy of other group members.

With a team, members need to interact with the other members so that whatever the team is trying to produce is significantly greater than the sum of individual contributions. In order for one team member to complete a task successfully, he or she may be dependent on another team member's expertise or interpersonal skills. The dependency that exists between and among team members is recognized as interdependence; the fact that the team's end result is more than the sum of its parts, and more than individuals could produce working separately, is known as *synergy*.

Observations From Team-Building Training

In our work in providing training for organizations as to how they might lead the development of higher performing teams, an interesting phenomenon frequently occurs. As facilitators, we will "create" teams right on the spot by assigning participants to a group. The particular activity that we ask participants to engage in requires that they individually formulate responses to a series of questions about a topic on which they typically know very little. The next step is to have the group, through a consensus process, come up with a group response for each item. The goal of the activity is to learn more about how groups and teams actually function. In this activity, we tend to declare the presence of synergy if the group response (total score) is equal to or better than the score of the best individual in the group. It is quite revealing to put a group of individuals together who may have never before worked together as a team and have them quantify that, together, they are better than individual effort. The way that we, as facilitators, create "teams" for this activity is not the way to go about creating real teams in real organizations, but this approach does work well in a training activity.

Occasionally, a single member may qualify under the category, "often wrong, but seldom in doubt." This individual may not know anything about the topic but is so strong in his or her arguments that other group members simply give in for the sake of harmony. Individuals who argue so strongly but lack expertise do the group a major disservice because their efforts revolve around getting their needs met as opposed to putting the team first. This runs counter to the power of identifying and using your talents.

Sometimes we will find a group member who does have some expertise in the topic that is used in the activity. This person may tell the others the "right" answer only one time. If the group displays low receptivity to her contributions, she may psychologically withdraw her membership from the group activity.

Other Differences

Two other factors that typically differentiate teams from groups are the presence of shared goal(s) and the presence of a shared accountability. In addition to interdependence, there are commonly understood goals about what the team is trying to accomplish and a collective responsibility for the accomplishment of these goals. This then results in a shared accountability. The team, together, is accountable. An individual is not accountable for the team's performance, the team is accountable. At the same time, with this shared accountability, if one member fails, the team fails. Groups that require interdependence, have shared goals, and have a shared accountability technically qualify as a team.

It has been my experience in most organizations that I have led, and many in which I have worked, that there is much rhetoric about commitment to the team approach. The reality, however, is that many have arrived at their position of leadership through individual achievement. A skilled leader must recognize that some people naturally prefer individual achievement to team accomplishment. This requires the leader to develop strong skills in developing teams and a team-based environment.

It is truly unfortunate, but in today's environment of bottom-line mentality—whether the bottom line is an increased financial profit statement or increased test scores on end-of-year and end-of-course tests in a school setting—I find employees who are starving for relationship building, a set of needs that are unmet in this ongoing age of accountability. The leadership lesson here is that leaders must balance task focus with relationship building. I cannot overstate my belief that, if we continue to focus on task completion without the balance of relationship building, we will continue to see more and more of our good people burn out, dropout, or psychologically opt out.

TEAM BUILDING REQUIRES EMPOWERMENT

The leader's role in creating a team-based environment involves the empowerment of team members. Empowerment actually means that it is the leader's responsibility to take the initiative to identify those conditions in his or her organization that are causing employees to feel that they are powerless and cannot influence the direction of the organization. Once the conditions have been identified, the leader should use the power of his or her office to remove the disempowering organizational practices. In recent years with our team building activities, we have frequently asked team members to identify the behaviors of leaders who empower others to act. Specifically, we have asked the following questions:

How do leaders empower others?

What do the leaders say or do?

What is the impact on subordinates?

Sample Descriptors Used by Followers Who Felt Empowered by Their Leaders

- Saw strengths in diversity
- Power was in listening
- Communicator
- Helped us reach our potential
- Linked the future to the past
- Allowed us to "color outside the lines"
- Created a safe environment in order to take risks
- Related to us on our level
- Never put anyone down
- Didn't care about credit
- Gave ownership
- Visionary
- Participated with us
- Built a strong sense of trust
- Humorous
- Creative
- Caring
- Committed
- Delegated effectively
- Shared responsibility
- Believed in us and then we believed in ourselves
- Was dissatisfied with the status quo
- Refused to use symbols of authority
- Validated the behaviors he liked
- Each person was made to feel important
- Every success counted

When team members feel empowered, they realize that the organization has a "people first" policy, and, therefore, they feel significant. Employees recognize that ongoing learning and competent performance are important parts of the culture. Employees feel that they are part of a community, and they find their work to be exciting.

CONCLUSION

Leaders of high-performing teams spend the necessary time *up front* in creating the team. In order to do this, they must possess the ability to identify and use their *own* talents, as well as the talents of those who will be a part of the team. Leaders must never lie to themselves, especially about their own strengths and weaknesses. Once they are honest about themselves, they can become better at staffing around their own shortcomings as a leader. Strive to be a leader who will seek to identify other players whose skills will complement your own. Selecting people who are much like you will result in comfortable communication, and you will probably get along well, but your performance will always be less than it could be if you identify and manage a diversity of talents. An important leadership skill for leading twenty-first-century organizations is the ability to manage diversity. This includes working with and managing people whose talents are significantly different from your own.

ENGAGING SELF AND OTHERS

The following activities and materials are designed to involve you, the reader, and others, as you and they create learning communities. Because our major emphasis in this book is on leadership lessons for adults, the exercises focus on adult learning.

Activity 2.2

List five adjectives that describe what you consider to be your strongest leadership skills/traits. Then indicate how you can use each of these traits to improve the performance of your organization.

Adjective   Use

_____   _____

_____   _____

_____   _____

_____   _____

_____   _____

Activity 2.3

Name three to five ways that your organization demonstrates that it highly values the identification and use of employee strengths.

_____

_____

_____

_____

Name three to five ways that your organization might improve its effort to identify and use employee strengths.

_____

_____

_____

_____

Activity 2.4

Make a list of the characteristics that describe the *best* team of which you have ever been a part.

_____   _____

_____   _____

_____   _____

List the characteristics that describe the behavior of the *leader* of this *best* team.

_____   _____

_____   _____

_____   _____

Activity 2.5

Think of a fellow team member whom you trust as much or more than you do any other team member. What behaviors does he or she exhibit that result in your trust?

_____

_____

_____

_____

What does a member of your team do to lead you to conclude that he or she is "playing politics" or "protecting his or her turf"?

_____

_____

_____

_____

If you were to have "fun" in your team meetings, what would the team be doing? What would _you_ be doing?

_____

_____

_____

_____

How would feedback from fellow team members help you? How would it help the team?

_____

_____

_____

_____

Activity 2.6

Complete the following:

When working together, my current team is most effective in the following areas:

_____

_____

_____

The major conflicts within my current team are:

_____

_____

_____

Activity 2.7

Think of a day you might identify as your personal best day at work. Your first task, with respect to this day, is to write in the left-hand column of the Talent Inventory that follows a chronology of this day from the time you got up in the morning until the time you went to sleep at night. The first item or two may read something like this: 6 A.M. got up; 6:15 A.M. showered and put on favorite outfit; 6:30 A.M. ate a good breakfast, and so on.

Your second task is to list in the second column the unique qualities (talents) you used in correspondence with the times you listed in the first column. Each of these qualities is a "tape" that goes off in your head when you encounter a particular situation. For example, 8:15 A.M. "I used my organizational skills to create an outline for the report I am writing."

Your third task is to name, in the third column, the source(s) of the tape (talent) you listed in the second column. These sources may include a parent or parents, a teacher, a religious figure, an aunt, an uncle, a grandparent, a mentor, or others. For example, a mentor may have introduced you to a software program that was helpful in organizing your report.

Your final task is to write in the fourth column your decision to either keep and act out the tape (talent), or reverse the tape and not act it out as you were originally intending to do it. In the case of organizational skills, you decided to organize your report as your mentor suggested. In another situation, your impulse might be to bark out orders in a dictatorial style, much as your first manager taught you to do, but you don't act out this tape because it would be counterproductive.

A TALENT INVENTORY

Chronology of an Ideal (Best) Day at Work	My Unique Qualities in This Day (Tapes)	Sources of These Tapes	Personal Decisions to Keep These Tapes (Act on Them)

Purpose Statement:

My purpose is to use my talents of _____,
_____, and _____ to support and
inspire others to identify and use their talents.

Note: After each person involved in this exercise has completed the talent inventory, it will probably be wise to have small group discussions with a recorder and reporter for each group. Reporters may then share with the larger group the results of small-group discussions.

Leadership Seminar Participant Responses:

Preparation skills.

Organizational skills.

Proactivity.

Follow-through.

The ability to be articulate, verbally and in writing.

A sense of humor.

The ability to motivate others to work together on committees.

Being a good team member.

Being firm but fair with others.

Activity 2.8a

One of the main findings of educators in completing the talent inventory in Activity 2.7 is the seemingly endless array of contradictions that face them. That is, they are expected to somehow reconcile opposing or mixed messages. Keeping in mind how you responded in doing the talent inventory, list several contradictions you have experienced at work:

_____

_____

_____

_____

_____

Leadership Seminar Participant Responses:

We are told that we are professionals, but we seem to be treated as bureaucrats—in part because of state regulation.

We are told that we are professionals with expertise, but outside consultants who know less than we do are hired.

We are told that the organization should display its accomplishments, and yet we should quietly go about our business.

We are told to think (plan) ahead and catch up (look backward).

We are told to be positive, but face the negative.

COMPLEMENTARY COMMENTARY

It is clear from responses to this exercise that contradictions are double edged. They are often a source of consternation, while at the same time a challenge that can bring out our creativity as leaders. How is this possible? Contradictions produce inner tension that awaken us from comfortable routines, traditions, and rituals. It is the contradictions that really bother us that force us to be proactive as leaders.

Some contradictions call for hard psychological work. Others are a cause for celebration, even though they also require different kinds of work—usually of a more technical nature. For example, you have recently hired a bright but outspoken person. You find this person interesting and helpful as new ideas are generated in the organization's day-to-day activities. At the same time, you recognize that others are bothered by this person's forthrightness—especially in meetings.

Activity 2.8b

List under each of the following headings those contradictions you celebrate and those on which you choose to do hard psychological work in order to reconcile.

Celebrate	Reconcile

Activity 2.9

This chapter identified four steps of team building. The first step was to identify your own talents, and the second step was to recognize the role of others who helped you identify and use such talents.

The third step consists of publicly acknowledging the role of others from your past in developing your talents. List the ways in which you have taken the third step in the team-building process and discuss what you have listed with others in your class or seminar setting.

_____

_____

_____

_____

The fourth step in the team-building process is to publicly recognize your appreciation for other team members' talents. List these talents and their contributors, after which you can share with each other what you have written.

_____

_____

_____

_____

CASE 2: Two Views of Approaching Talent Deficits

You are a member of a three-person discussion panel at a convention on effective leadership. Approximately one hundred people are in the audience. The first speaker on the panel presents her view of effective leadership: "The secret in becoming an effective leader is to feed your strengths and starve your weaknesses." This speaker develops this thesis (big idea) at some length, giving examples of famous people who have lived this philosophy. The second speaker, obviously worked up by his predecessor, responds as follows: "I can't disagree more! If you simply starve your weaknesses, you never develop latent talents that can be of benefit to others and yourself. It is by screwing up your courage and seeking to improve those things that you presently identify as weaknesses that you learn what you are capable of doing and, at the same time, you serve as a model for others who are reluctant to work through their weaknesses." You are the third and final speaker on the panel. What will you say?

_____

_____

_____

_____

_____

_____

Authors' Recommendations

A certain "culture" of panel discussion must be understood so that you don't consciously violate the norms or unwritten rules of discourse. The stated, or ideal, purpose of this event is the presentation and discussion of different points of view or interpretations of an issue so that the audience can be better informed, thus making better decisions in their lives and work worlds. It is also assumed that the panel members are open minded enough to learn from each other. In order for this purpose to be fulfilled, it is assumed that panel members will be civil and not personally attack each other.

Once again, this is the idealized description of a panel discussion. Audiences, especially in this television and computer age, have come to expect some "sizzle" as panel members present their views and confront each other. As a result, some panel discussions violate the boundaries of civility.

It is your challenge to listen carefully to the two previous speakers and probably take some notes to which you can speak in presenting your own views. It is both wise and civil to acknowledge the views of the two previous speakers before stating your own position. It is important to state your view with conviction and commitment because the audience will be reading your energy level as well as the content of your message.

SELF INVENTORY

Now that you have completed the readings and activities on "The Power of Identifying and Using Your Talents," think about what you've learned and respond to the following items on a five-point scale: 1 (low) to 5 (high).

1. My ability to assess my own talents candidly. _____

2. My general assessment of my effectiveness in using my talents. _____

3. My ability to assess the talents of those I lead candidly. _____

4. My general assessment of my effectiveness in helping others identify their talents. _____

5. My general assessment of my effectiveness in helping others use their talents. _____

6. The extent to which I welcome persons who have talents like my own to team situations. _____

7. The extent to which I welcome persons who have talents different from my own to team situations. _____

8. The extent to which I publicly acknowledge the role others have played in the development of my talents. _____

9. The extent to which I publicly acknowledge the talents of predecessors when I enter a new setting. _____

10. My competence in bringing on board persons new to the setting. _____

Note: If you are in a group setting, form discussion groups in order to share and summarize findings.

Scoring for Self Inventory
   Total the ratings and find your score in the following scale:

41–50	Superior
31–40	Above Average
21–30	Average
11–20	Below Average
0–10	Poor

SUGGESTED READINGS

Brubaker, D. L. (2004). *Creative Curriculum Leadership: Inspiring and Empowering Your School Community.* Thousand Oaks, CA: Corwin Press.

Conroy, P. (2003). *My Losing Season.* Garden City, NJ: Doubleday.

Levinson, D., & Levinson, J. (1997). *The Seasons of a Woman's Life.* New York: Random House.

Steinem, G. (1992). *Revolution From Within: A Book of Self-Esteem.* Boston: Little, Brown.

3

The Power of Learning

Dale L. Brubaker

At the onset of summer, children and adults dragged any lawn equipment available to the softball field behind our vacation cabins. After cutting the wild hay and weeds, we used flat fireplace wood to mark the bases, pitcher's mound, and home plate. At the end of the day, we gathered together all interested players and started our first game of the season.

The hardest part of each game was choosing sides. The two captains entered into a ritual known to anyone who has ever played ball: the bat was tossed to one captain who grabbed it with one hand; the second captain then placed his hand above his opponent's hand, and this was repeated until the captain who had the very top of the bat got first choice of players.

Players were chosen until one poor soul was left. "You take him, I don't want him," was the refrain of the captain with the last choice. "I don't either," was the response. "OK, I guess you can play with us," was how the matter was usually settled.

For several summers, Billy was the last player chosen due to his small size and lack of athletic ability. This was especially discouraging to Billy because his two sisters were bigger and stronger than he was. As teams were forming, they were chosen early.

A period of 30 years passed before I saw Billy again. He had married, moved out west, divorced, and returned home. After years of helpful therapy, Bill was a new man. He had listened to self-help tapes, bulked up in exercise clubs, and gained enough confidence to take on the world. He showed up at our cabin's doorstep with a greeting and an invitation: "Want to play ball?" My teenage children and I accepted, and off we went to the ball field where others had already gathered.

After teams were chosen, the game began; I couldn't believe the action that unfolded. Billy exerted himself in every department of the game of softball. He swung the bat with great force, sometimes hitting the ball. He played shortstop with an aggressiveness that knocked over the first baseman with throws to the bag. But Billy's intensity was most visible when he ran the bases. He knocked over everybody in his way. All I could think of was the proverbial "bull in the china shop." Everyone, save one, played a relaxed, fun game. Billy, however, had returned to rewrite history.

He had learned a good deal since he played softball as a boy, but he hadn't learned that it doesn't work to try to change the past. What will work is learning from the past and applying this knowledge in present-day contexts that are appropriate. The game that Billy was playing was largely in his own head.

The "Billy Syndrome" is understandable because it is within each of us. Billy's pain in being the last one chosen is one we have all experienced in some way at some time. We have for one reason or another been excluded. And our attempt to deal with this pain by rewriting history is best captured in the classic story of returning to a class reunion to prove to others (and ourselves) that we have, after all, amounted to something.

On occasion, we want to return to an earlier job or an earlier career choice only to find that times and situations have changed and that we can't, after all, make amends for past difficulties. Knowing this, we recognize that we can't rewrite history but we can celebrate the changes that have taken place in each of us and move on with our lives in constructive and personally satisfying directions.

True learning often involves a good deal of pain. We are forced to reach within ourselves to find something that will help us survive. What we find will be different for each person. Terry Anderson, a survivor of six and a half years as a prisoner in Lebanon, shares his story in his book, *Den of Lions,* and in his speeches to university students. In returning to Lebanon after his release, he expected his captors to apologize for the pain they had brought upon him and other captives. They didn't! Anderson discovered that he had to do the work of relating to the anger within himself. He essentially learned to do the hard work of letting go of the anger, rather than wearing it as a protective mantle. As a result, his story is one of liberation and learning.

Gloria Steinem describes a similar journey in her book aptly titled *Revolution From Within.* Although widely recognized for success in the external revolution for women's rights, she had not connected that progress with her internal spirit and consciousness. In learning to treat herself as well as she treated her best friends, she celebrated the words of Ernest Hemingway in *A Farewell to Arms:* "The world breaks everyone, and afterward, some are strong at the broken places."[1]

Terry Anderson, Gloria Steinem, and other effective leaders have come to the place where they recognize the power of learning. It is, indeed, a leadership lesson that lasts a lifetime.

Implications for Leaders

Larry D. Coble

ORIENTATION

In my experience I have known many leaders who, once they initially "arrived," had their careers stall or stop. In fact, considerable research suggests that, although individuals may appear to possess similar characteristics in terms of intelligence, drive, and ambition, some are able to stay on track while others derail. In this case, we are defining derailment as having a position that you want to keep and losing it, or not being able to get a position to which you aspire.

Some leaders have their responsibilities reduced; some are forced to take early retirement; some hit the glass ceiling; and some are fired. What is going on here is that those who are able to stay on track and avoid derailment are leaders who have become perpetual learners. Not only do they learn more from their experiences than those who derail, but they are also able to figure out how they are learning from their experiences so that they are able to learn more and more and at faster rates.

THE ONGOING LEARNER: REFLECTION ON EXPERIENCE

How do leaders become perpetual ongoing learners? They do so by reflecting on past practices. Perhaps the most distinguishing characteristic that separates leaders who are able to stay on track versus those who derail is that those who stay on track are able to learn more from their past experience by reflecting on the experience. They then mentally formulate leadership lessons that they have learned as a result of that reflection.

In multi-day leadership development programs, we often suggest that participants keep a reflective learning journal as a tool for taking charge of their own development. We are quick to point out that the journal is not to be a diary but, in fact, a journal. The guidelines that we recommend are fairly simple in concept but, if implemented properly, pay invaluable dividends. Much of my own growth and career planning has come as a result of having kept a reflective learning journal. The guidelines that we recommend are as follows:

Guidelines for the Reflective Learning Journal

- Reflect on those leadership challenges that demanded *most of your time and energy* for a set period of time. A good place to begin is by looking at the previous work week.
- Make no more than *one entry per week.*

- Make each entry *no more than one page in length.*
- In the first paragraph or two, capture the essence of the leadership challenge. The remainder of the entry should *include those leadership activities in which you engaged in addressing the challenge that worked for you; activities that failed; lessons that you learned; and whether or not you would do the same thing or something different if you faced similar challenges again.*

Analyzing Your Reflections

Over time, with continued reflection, you will begin to see trends that are present in strategies that work for you, as well as potential flaws that are getting in the way of successfully handling the challenges. One developmental opportunity here is to analyze your own successes and the successes of other effective leaders and retain those strategies.

As strange as it may sound, however, our achievements, although helpful up to a point, are not critical in our growth and development. *The true and more powerful developmental opportunity lies in those experiences that take on a negative connotation or might even be viewed as a failure at the time.* Learning from these "less than successful" experiences requires reflection on the experience. Consider what happened and how it unfolded. What were the roles that others played?

In our seminars, when we ask developing leaders to use one-word descriptors that describe their feelings when encountering life events that have shaped them both personally and professionally, we often get responses such as these:

• Anger	• Pain
• Fear	• Hurt
• Devastated	• Helplessness
• Anxiety	• Overwhelmed
• Frustration	• Stress

If leaders go through these experiences and reflect on them and learn from them, these experiences become developmental in nature. It is through reflection on the experience that most developing leaders come to the conclusion that what started out as something negative can become a very powerful learning experience over time and can evolve to something very positive. The power of learning involves coming face to face with the terms of our failures and mistakes.

IMPLICATIONS OF EXPERIENCES

Let's consider your career and the developmental implications of experiences that are less than positive. Effective leadership development demands that you take on challenges that will almost certainly expose your weaknesses or developmental needs. As long as you stay in jobs that are comfortable and do not require a "stretch," you are doing yourself a major disservice. The opportunity for your growth and development is a career that includes a variety of leadership challenges paired with feedback on your performance and reflection on all of this.

Many leaders, if given the opportunity, will take on only those jobs where they know they can be successful, ultimately staying in their personal comfort zones. Even if we want to get out of our comfort zones, it does not come easy. The way we have been shaped causes us to encounter a type of built-in personal inertia and to continue to use the same strategies for being successful that we have always used and that work for us most of the time.

We know, however, that highly effective leaders who perform at peak levels take on challenges leading to new insights. They make a conscious choice: their development is more important than remaining comfortable. They tend to be driven by compelling internal goals, which they have set for themselves, that are higher than any goals an organization or boss will set for them. These kinds of jobs, with key challenges that tend to cause leaders to stretch, are developmental experiences; through reflection, they result in powerful learning opportunities. In this process, highly effective leaders are relentless self-questioners. They become their own best teachers.

ADVANTAGES OF BECOMING YOUR OWN "BEST TEACHER"

Before becoming involved in a number of activities to help you become a reflective learner, reviewing some principles and concepts that are basic to this approach will be helpful.

- Your learning is experiential; you learn by doing or, more aptly put, by what you have done.
- Your "school" has no walls or barriers. It is limited only to your personal experiences.
- Your "curriculum" is based on life-long experiences, from the day you were born to now.

> You can learn from experiences that took place long ago, as well as those that happened just moments ago.

> You can be involved in *continuing life-long education.*

> You can benefit from either personal or professional experiences.

> You probably will learn more from your failures than your successes. Your most horrible fiasco might well be the best thing that ever happened to you.

> Your failure might be related to organizational and environmental conditions over which you have no control.

Your chances of becoming a responsible independent learner and worker are increased measurably.

Your learning is primarily self-directed, but you have the freedom to receive counsel and advice.

Your efforts to improve may be a private matter or shared with others.

You are accountable for your own improvement or lack thereof.

And, finally, through this process of reflective learning, you will become a more effective leader and, moreover, be in a better position to assist those who have the same goal.

PRINCIPLES AND PROCEDURES INVOLVED IN SUCCESSFUL LEARNING FROM YOUR OWN EXPERIENCE

- Benefit from both success and failures. Don't get too cocky about successes or too devastated by failures.
- Be realistic and honest in analyzing failures. Admit your own deficiencies and mistakes, but don't hesitate to raise questions with the organization, leadership, conditions, and associates when that judgment is warranted.
- Take on jobs and tasks that are outside of your comfort zone. Routine application does little to promote learning. But be cautious in taking on assignments in which there is a very high probability of failure, unless all—bosses, peers, and self—fully understand that failure might occur but that much can be learned from failure.
- Learn to monitor yourself when you are performing critical tasks. Ask such questions as, "Am I overexerting myself? Should I call in reinforcements? Am I taking this job too seriously?"
- In analyzing performance, focus more on why something happened rather than what happened.
- Invite a trusted colleague to provide you with an honest appraisal of how you behave on the job.
- Keep in mind that there are numerous ways to attack a problem. Avoid sticking with one learning preference, but adapt your style to conditions associated with the problem.
- Contrast feelings, actions, and behaviors in your current job to ones that were experienced in past jobs.
- Think way beyond the current task. Ask yourself, "Will this experience lead to desirable possibilities and opportunities for the organization, the personnel, and myself?"
- Being fired is not necessarily a disaster. To be fired in certain situations is a compliment.

- Use both retrospective (reflections on past experiences) and prospective (planning future learning) learning to bring about personal growth.
- Strive to understand the world both inside and outside your organization.
- Relate present and future to past.
- Become involved in a variety of leadership experiences and challenges.

ENGAGING SELF AND OTHERS

The following activities and materials are designed to involve you, the reader, and others, as you and they create learning communities. Because our major emphasis in this book is on leadership lessons for adults, the exercises focus on adult learning.

Activity 3.1

Reflect on the significant learning activities in which you were involved in the last 10 years. Identify the most profitable and least profitable of those you experienced. Record the factors that you believe contributed to your worst learning experience. Now do the same for the best experience. Compare the factors associated with the best and least helpful experiences.

Best Experience

_____

_____

_____

_____

Least Helpful Experience

_____

_____

_____

_____

Activity 3.2
ADJECTIVE CHECKLIST

Survey of Emotional Reactions to Profound Childhood, Adolescent, and Adulthood Learning Experiences

List some of your childhood, adolescent, and adulthood learning experiences, either successes or mistakes.

CHILDHOOD LEARNING EXPERIENCE

_____

_____

_____

ADOLESCENT LEARNING EXPERIENCE

_____

_____

_____

ADULTHOOD LEARNING EXPERIENCE

_____

_____

_____

For each of the experiences you listed, indicate with a check (✓) the emotions that you felt during the time you were involved with the experience. Review response patterns to determine whether your reactions for each experience were mainly favorable or unfavorable and whether there were similarities among the emotions experienced at the three age levels.

Emotional Responses	Childhood	Adolescence	Adulthood
1. Stress			
2. Rejected			
3. Pain			
4. Pessimism			
5. Fear			
6. Calm			
7. Anger			
8. Understanding			
9. Success			
10. Failure			
11. Guilt			
12. Love			
13. Tension			
14. Confidence			
15. Optimism			
16. Pleasure			
17. Appreciated			
List other emotional responses			
18.			
19.			
20.			
21.			
22.			
23.			
24.			
25.			

Activity 3.3

We suspect that organizational leaders know more about how adults learn than they think they do. With this in mind, please list what you know about how adults learn:

_____

_____

_____

_____

_____

Leadership Seminar Participant Responses:

> There is no one kind of intelligence, but rather there are many different kinds of intelligence. [See Howard Gardner. (1983). *Frames of Mind: The Theory of Multiple Intelligences.* New York: Basic Books. Gardner identifies 8 distinct intelligences: (1) linguistic; (2) logical-mathematical; (3) spatial; (4) bodily kinesthetic; (5) musical; (6) interpersonal; (7) intrapersonal, to know oneself; and (8) naturalist, to discriminate in the natural world.]

> Adult learning is based on the construction of knowledge. [An adult must own learning by connecting it with frames of reference and experience.]

> By sharing with others what one has learned (teaching), an adult learns at an even deeper level.

> Personal developmental learning varies from adult learner to adult learner. There is no one set stage for all adults to learn this or that. [See L.S. Vygotsky. (1978). *Mind in Society: The Development of Higher Psychological Processes.* Cambridge, MA: Harvard University Press.]

> Adults are challenged to learn in a world that is increasingly complex and fast-moving—a world that is rapidly changing "the rules of the game." [See R.D. Putnam. (2000). *Bowling Alone: The Collapse and Revival of American Community.* New York: Simon & Schuster.]

> Adults learn best when invited to use their talents. [See D. L. Brubaker. (2004). *Creative Curriculum Leadership.* Thousand Oaks, CA: Corwin Press.]

> Active involvement within real-life situations is a major key to effective adult learning.

Activity 3.4

This exercise is a check of your answers to Activity 3.1. Think for a moment about a time in your life when you experienced being part of a learning community at its best—a true learning community. Identify the characteristics of this learning community:

_____

_____

_____

_____

How do items in this list compare and contrast with your answers in Activity 3.1?

_____

_____

_____

_____

Activity 3.5

All organizations are vulnerable to fads—temporary fashions that serve as "the flavor of the month." These panaceas, a kind of magic hope, litter the landscape along which organizations travel. This parade of programs, often initiated by newly appointed leaders who want to make a name for themselves, marches by in dramatic fashion, but their throwaway nature is clearly noted by those who have to clean up. The point of all of this for our discussion of adult learning is simply that fads work against true learning.

Which of the following four responses do you usually adopt when a "bureaucratic superior" introduces a reform effort that you clearly identify as a fad?

- ❑ Be a true believer—the show will make a positive difference.
- ❑ Wave the flag and join in, knowing full well that the show is everything to your leader(s)—not to you.
- ❑ Don't be obvious about not participating, for this, too, will pass.
- ❑ Take the "boss" aside and share your reservations about the fad.

List the fads that you have been expected to implement in the various organizations in which you have served:

_____

_____

_____

Finally, what is your position as a leader with regard to the introduction of fads in contrast to longer-lasting reform efforts? In other words, what will your position be on the firing line with regard to this matter?

_____

_____

_____

Leadership Seminar Participant Responses:

Involve your staff in researching programs and materials with an eye on quality and durability.

Finances are a real issue. What, from among the useful, can we afford?

Give attention to the angle of trajectory of the proposed reform. "What from this reform, if anything, will be here in 10 or 20 years?"

Ask the question, "In whose interest is this proposed reform?" In other words, "Who will benefit from this reform?"

What are my learning needs with regard to this reform? What are my political needs with respect to this reform?

CASE 3: The Challenge in Being the Chief Learning Officer

Your high credibility as a quick study and person interested in keeping up with new ideas has earned you the informal title of Chief Learning Officer (CLO) in your organization. You have somewhat mixed reactions to this informal title given the kinds of challenges associated with it.

First, although you are fortunate that the head of the organization values your contribution as CLO, you are also aware that some, if not many, in the organization tend to discount what you do because few tangible products result from your efforts. You are, in effect, a person more interested in process than product, in long-term progress rather than short-term, highly visible results—often of a quick-fix nature. How will you relate to this matter?

_____

_____

_____

Second, you know that those who support the quick fix are often optimists who choose to overlook the tremendous effort and even pain that accompany learning. In other words, they choose to believe that things will naturally work themselves out in a positive way. You, on the other hand, are always hopeful, but you also know that important learning often involves making mistakes and learning from them—a painful experience, to be sure. How will you deal with optimists like those just described?

_____

_____

_____

Third, you have learned that change and conservation go hand-in-hand in an organization. For some things to change, other things have to remain the same. You face two extreme positions in some persons in your organization—those who seem to be stuck in tradition and resist most, if not all, change, and those who seem to thrive on change without honoring those things that have worked well in the past. How will you relate to persons in these two extreme positions?

_____

_____

_____

_____

Fourth, and finally, you believe that learning has both a personal and an organizational face. What strategies will you employ in order to help others see the relationship between personal and organizational learning?

_____

_____

_____

_____

Authors' Recommendations

The content of your commitments is stated in the four points in this case. You must be clear as to your role in the organization and your overall purpose in fulfilling this role.

You are not the CEO (Chief Executive Officer), but rather you serve as the CLO (Chief Learning Officer). Your purpose is to engage members of the organization in learning activities that are consistent with the organizational vision that has come into being under the leadership of the CEO and others. Members of the organization will read your authenticity and commitment to the learning process and its relationship to stated and operationalized goals of the organization. They will give attention to how you will react when contradictions emerge between learning goals and actual practices. Two kinds of criticisms or pitfalls are facing you: (1) you are at fault for the views that you hold; and/or (2) you say one thing and you do another. The first pitfall can be addressed by simply saying that differences of views are essential to the learning process, for indeed there is no movement or learning without some friction. The second pitfall can erode your credibility and even bring about your downfall, for it can lead to your being called duplicitous and a "phony."

SELF INVENTORY

Now that you have completed the readings and activities on "The Power of Learning," think about what you've learned and respond to the following items on a five-point scale: 1 (low) to 5 (high).

1. The value I place on my own learning.   _____

2. The extent to which my organization will recognize   _____
   and reward me for the value I place on my own learning.

3. The value I place on organizational learning.   _____

4. The extent to which my organization will recognize and
    reward me for the value I place on organizational learning.   _____

5. The extent to which I believe that hard work is a part of learning.   _____

6. The extent to which I believe that making some mistakes is
    part of learning.   _____

7. The extent to which I believe that pain sometimes
    accompanies learning life's lessons.   _____

8. The extent to which I believe that "breakdowns"
    can lead to "breakthroughs."   _____

9. The extent to which I believe that there are multiple
    intelligences within each person.   _____

10. The extent to which I act as though there are
    multiple intelligences within each person.   _____

Note: If you are in a group setting, form discussion groups in order to share and summarize findings.

Scoring for Self Inventory

Total the ratings and find your score in the following scale:

41–50	Superior
31–40	Above Average
21–30	Average
11–20	Below Average
0–10	Poor

SUGGESTED READINGS

Fullan, M. (2001). *Leading in a Culture of Change.* San Francisco: Jossey-Bass.

Norris, C., Barnett, B., Basom, M., & Yerkes, D. (2002). *Developing Educational Leaders, A Working Model: The Learning Community in Action.* New York: Teachers College Press.

Putnam, R. D. (2000). *Bowling Alone: The Collapse and Revival of American Community.* New York: Simon & Schuster.

Roberts, S. M., & Pruitt, E. Z. (2003). *Schools as Professional Learning Communities: Collaborative Activities and Strategies for Professional Development.* Thousand Oaks, CA: Corwin Press.

4

The Power of Competence

Dale L. Brubaker

It's 11 A.M. and a loyal customer of 10 years walks up to the reception desk at a quick-lube business. "I need an oil change," he remarks. The receptionist responds in an apologetic way, "I'm sorry, but nobody showed up for work today." The customer looks at the six empty bays in the lube station, shakes his head, and drives to a different lube business a mile down the road.

An elementary-school teacher is teaching fractions—incorrectly. The children's examples in the textbook are correct. A child points out to the teacher that the example on the board is incorrect. The teacher—flustered and defensive—says, "I was just testing you to see if you knew the right answer."

After much thought and attention to his financial situation, a new car buyer walks into a dealership ready to make a purchase. But he first needs to ask questions about the particular model in which he is interested. The sales representative responds, "I'm sorry. The person who really knows this product isn't in right now."

A 60-year-old diabetic woman in a rural area visits her doctor who tells her that she must have her legs amputated in order to survive. She has been taught not to question authority in general and physicians in particular. Her son, however, drives her to a well-known university medical center where her condition is evaluated and alternative treatments are initiated. Today, twenty years after her own doctor said she would never walk again, she is walking on her own legs.

Everyone has stories similar to these. They illustrate the power of incompetence. At the same time, there are plenty of stories about the power of competence. The interesting thing about both kinds of stories is the emotion brought to the storytelling itself—an emotion clearly evident in our nonverbal communication. The message is that competence and incompetence really matter in our lives!

A TOUGH LOOK IN THE MIRROR

It's relatively easy to identify competence and incompetence in others. It's more difficult to identify competence and incompetence in ourselves. I ask participants in leadership seminars to draw a vertical line down the center of a piece of paper with "Competencies" heading the left column and "Incompetencies" heading the right column. They are then asked to list their own personal competencies and incompetencies.

As might be expected, balance—or lack of balance—between the two columns is an expression of the participant's attitudes and behaviors, particularly his or her "presentation of self." In general, people tend to underrate their ability to do things well.

Occasionally, however, there are some participants whose "competencies" column simply doesn't have enough space. Yet in the course of the seminar, it's obvious that the attitudes and behaviors they exhibit directly contradict the accuracy of their written competencies. For example, a person may say, "I'm a good listener." Yet he or she demonstrates during the day that this is simply not true.

How Can One Relate to
Competency Inflation in Self and Others?

The first dimension of this challenge is awareness. Such lack of awareness was graphically, and somewhat humorously, brought to my attention some years ago when I was a member of a small church group that sat around a kitchen table each Sunday morning. Each of us was—in our own mind—an expert on "the law" whenever the subject arose. In fact, we had varying levels of "bull," from low-class bull to high-class bull.

One Sunday, we were joined by an attorney who really *did* know the law. All members of the group—except one—were relatively quiet that day when legal issues were discussed. The lone dissenter simply didn't know what he didn't know. Although the attorney talked about contract law, the dissenter thought he had said "covenant law," and our group was treated to a five-minute lecture on the intricacies of covenant law—a subject known only to the dissenter himself. When a member of the group said he thought there was a distinction between unofficial covenants of a spiritual nature and legal contracts, the dissenter replied "Whatever . . ." and continued with his lecture.

Most members of the group had wry smiles on their faces. The attorney, bless his heart, said nothing.

We've all done it. We simply try to prove we're competent when we aren't. The problem is twofold: it steals resources that might better be used to acquire the competency we don't have, and others know that we're faking it anyway.

It's also true that pretending to be someone we aren't can be very costly to the organization. Stories about malpractice and faulty products are legendary. Lawsuits are frequently part of the stories.

When our family goes to the beach, I like to get up each morning and go to the pier. I always find interesting characters fishing, drinking coffee, and talking. It's a fun-loving group who seem to be there as much for the social interaction as anything else.

One of my favorite characters is a retired executive who alternates days of fishing and playing golf. One day, I sidled up to his fishing spot and asked, "Ted, tell me the biggest problems you've had in managing people." He looked at me carefully and responded: "Three questions: What do you do with a motivated imbecile? And what do you do with someone who always says 'no' even when he agrees with you?"

"That's only two questions," I said. He quickly added, "What do you do with a person who interrupts your fishing with stupid questions?"

Ted's response reminded me that one of his main competencies is to cut to the chase so that he can focus on what's really important to him at the time—in this case, fishing, rather than talking to an inquisitive writer.

Implications for Leaders

Larry D. Coble

ORIENTATION

Being competent is what matters most in determining your effectiveness as a leader. In fact, you can't truly be considered a leader unless you are viewed to be competent by your peers, your boss, and your direct reports. This idea of competence as a leader encompasses many aspects of leadership. Certain basic leadership competencies are required for success, regardless of the position and the leadership challenge. For example, it's already been established that, in order to be successful and avoid derailment, leaders must be highly skilled in their ability to work with people. When I led large complex organizations, I would often find myself telling my senior staff that I could "buy" all the technical assistance I needed but that what I really needed was people who demonstrated the leadership capacity to work with all kinds of people, people who saw the world differently from the way they viewed the world. A very important lesson is to recognize that, as a leader, you need to surround yourself with people who *complement* your strengths and not those who necessarily possess all the same strengths that you possess. Competence involves understanding that if you have a staff who thinks just like you think, you will frequently come to agreement quickly, but the decision-making process will be much less creative than it could have been with diverse points of view represented on your staff.

Another basic leadership competency that is imperative in any role is that of effective communicator. Much has been written about the importance of being able to communicate effectively if you are going to lead effectively. What is often understated is that effective communication includes the ability to *truly listen* to what others are saying. I once read an article that suggested that to be effective we have to listen with "three ears." We need to listen to what people are saying; we need to listen to what they aren't saying; and we need to listen to what they want to say but don't know how. I believe that communication experts would agree that the real power in effective communication is in developing the ability to listen. Most people are so preoccupied with what they are going to say next that they really don't hear what another person is saying. They don't pay attention to the body language, and they don't listen to the pauses and consider what is going on behind the verbiage. I personally have never known an excellent leader who was not also an excellent communicator.

FEEDBACK IS THE "BREAKFAST OF CHAMPIONS"

Please understand that even world-class leaders don't exhibit mastery of every leadership competency. It has been my experience, and there is considerable research to prove it, that most leaders have two, three, or more areas that need to be addressed to enhance their effectiveness in their current position. When giving feedback to hundreds of practicing leaders, it is rare to find one who does not have a "best developmental" opportunity. Our typical approach includes the use of 360-degree feedback. This type of feedback is critical to one's leadership development because it provides for the use of multi-raters and allows the leader to view her own performance against a set of leadership criteria and compare her view to how her peers, her boss, and her direct reports see her. What makes this feedback even more powerful is that all rater responses, excluding the leader's own responses, include which competencies are most necessary for success in the current job. Those that are most important, but are the competencies in which the leader is least skilled, represent the leader's most pressing need for leadership development.

A major implication for leaders is to realize that, once you move beyond the requirement of basic leadership competencies, it is critical to realize that the skill set that helps you *get* a position may not be the skill set that helps you *keep* the position. For example, you may be promoted because of your strengths around working with details. As you take on more and more responsibility as a leader, however, the new role may require that most of your time be spent managing others who are working with the details, and that your success now rests with your ability to conceptualize a direction for your department, division, your school system, or corporation.

Perpetual Learners, Relentless Self-Questioners

Highly effective leaders are perpetual learners; they never stop learning and growing. A proven tactic for ongoing growth is to become a relentless self-questioner. As a leader, you should regularly ask yourself, why did I do what I did? This approach will be particularly helpful when you handle a situation less than effectively. Pay attention to what you did and why you did it. Was it a habit? Was it a challenge that looked so much like something you had handled before that you saw too much sameness in the situation, but in the final analysis the circumstances weren't that similar?

In our previous work with leaders who have derailed versus those who have stayed on track, we learned that those who tend to stay on track seek out and respond to feedback. In addition to their own self-perceptions, they wanted to know how others in the organization felt about their performance. It is the classic, "how am I doing?" idea. They took the feedback one additional step. Those who benefited most from the feedback accepted it in the spirit in which it was intended—a response to an honest question that, if addressed, would make the leader more effective. They then tried to address the deficiency. Leaders use feedback in nondefensive ways to become better leaders.

COMPETENCE VERSUS INCOMPETENCE

Over the past 30-plus years, I have led four large complex organizations and one small consulting group, and I have worked for two other organizations. During my tenure, I have been passionately interested in seeing these organizations—for which I have worked and which I have led—succeed. It is my belief that in order for the organizations to have success, the individuals within those organizations have to be successful as team players and as individual achievers. To attain this kind of success, the formal leader must ensure his own development and create conditions for those under his leadership to continue to develop to their highest potential. Through my experiences in leading and "organization watching," along with the practical application of research on highly effective leaders, I have developed a list of characteristics that, in my mind, capture issues around competence and incompetence and, in turn, introduce some of the major learnings and actions that are pertinent for success as a leader. The list is not exhaustive; it assumes technical competence for any given leadership role.

Competent Leaders	Incompetent Leaders
Nurture subordinates, attempt to meet their needs, and provide psychological support.	Ignore the needs of the people in the organization.
Put people first.	Put tasks and paper before people.
Use power and authority constructively to advance the goals of the organization and help people become successful.	Use power and authority destructively to advance personal goals at the expense of the organization and the people in it.
Understand the importance of past significance, including slogans, symbols, rituals, and ceremonies and the emotional attachment that people in the organization hold for these aspects of their culture.	Fail to recognize the importance of past significance of slogans, symbols, rituals, and ceremonies and the emotional attachment people feel for these elements of their culture; act like history began the day they "rode into town."
Have a strong ego.	Are arrogant.
Have experienced a wide array of life and leadership experiences commensurate with their current level of responsibility.	Have been "fast tracked" to the point that their developmental experiences are inadequate for the position at which they have arrived.
Have developed strong political skills.	Are politically naïve.
Grant trust before subordinates earn it.	Betray the trust of others.
Will not tolerate financial mismanagement and budget irregularities.	Tend to be so removed from the financial side of the operation they are solely dependent on the word of others.
Are flexible change leaders.	Are inflexible and unwilling or unable to adapt to positive change.
Can adapt to a new boss and understand the executive culture.	Have difficulty in adapting to a new boss and the executive culture.
Develop the ability to learn from their experiences through reflection on past experiences.	Are not good reflective practitioners; fail to learn and grow from past experiences, especially those that they handled less effectively.

COMPETENCE IS IN THE EYE OF THE BEHOLDER

Leaders who stay on track through constructive productivity and get what they want for their organizations and themselves are competent. Competency, however, is like beauty. Up to a point, it is in the eye of the beholder. If enough people perceive you to be competent, then you will be considered competent. If enough people or the "right" people perceive you to be incompetent, then you will be considered incompetent. In order to actually enhance your competence and the perception that you are competent, consider the following guidelines:

Be As Good As Your Word

Competent people do what they say they are going to do. If you make a promise, then keep it. This approach will always help you develop trust. The cumulative effect, over time, of you doing what you say you are going to do will create a culture in which your people will feel that the boss is as good as her word. It's not only hard, it's impossible to be competent if you can't create a climate of trust in which to lead.

Follow Up and Follow Through

I have known many leaders who attained reasonable success pretty much on their ability to get organized, meet timelines, and hold themselves and those around them accountable. There are multitudes of leaders and aspiring leaders who can "talk a good game." The significant difference, however, is in the ones who actually deliver. You cannot deliver as a leader unless you take personal responsibility for either doing or overseeing the necessary follow-up to get things going and brought to closure. You do this through a balance of attention to people and tasks.

Do More Than Is Required

One of the distinguishing characteristics that I have always looked for when deciding whether or not to promote a developing leader to an area of greater responsibility is his or her track record of going the extra mile. Leaders who are willing to make the commitments of additional time and energy create outcomes that serve the organization and their own development well. You want your boss and your subordinates to view you as someone who will exceed the requirements of a particular job. If you do more than is required, and you do this well, it will place you among a very elite group of extremely competent leaders.

Develop Big Picture Skills

The higher you move in any organization, the more important big-picture skills become. You may have been hired because you had technical skills that were to be applied at lower levels of the organization, but successful personal development and/or upward mobility require that you develop the ability to see the big picture. Inherent in this process is helping those you lead understand "connections." You won't be able to explain connections unless you can see the big picture and how everything fits together. With big-picture skills, you will be able to explain the reasons behind events that occur in the organization, and you will be able to help people better understand their individual roles in making the organization successful.

Learn to View Your Organization Through "New" Lenses, Not Just the Way You Normally Prefer to View Life in Your Organization

The reality is this: We really don't see the organization as it is; we see the organization as we are. And we are a collection of genetic predispositions and life experiences. We interpret life in our organizations based on who we are and how we have been shaped. I can guarantee that the organization looks very different if you are on the factory floor as compared to being the chief executive officer, or if you are a school bus driver as compared to being the school superintendent. Highly effective leaders can reframe organizational events and see them through eyes that they would not normally use. This leadership skill enables leaders to relate to all aspects of the organization.

Be Ambitious, But Not Too Ambitious

I would never want a developing leader working for me who was not ambitious. By ambition, I am suggesting that the leader can be ambitious to do an outstanding job with an assignment or she or he can be ambitious to develop her or his leadership capacity for more organizational responsibilities and upward mobility opportunities. A leader can be ambitious in his or her present assignment and not strive for promotion, or he or she can be ambitious working for a promotion. The key implication for leaders is not to be ambitious at the expense of others. If your staff begins to feel that you are trying to advance your own ambitions at their expense or the expense of the organization, the results will be an internal political struggle that will make it nearly impossible for you to do your job effectively.

Procrastination Is a Problem for Everybody, Especially the Boss

Few things have bothered me more over my career than direct reports who would put off doing something that was important. Psychologists tell us that the root of procrastination is poor self-image. I believe that there is a lot of truth in this. Of course, I understand that you can have a great self-image and be so busy that something important fails to get done. In this case, the real issue may not be procrastination; it may be the inability to choose among tasks, all of which are very important. If this is the case, it still *looks* like procrastination to the boss. Whatever the reason, don't put off something that is viewed to be very important, especially to the boss. Work late, work nights, work weekends if necessary, but get it done. No excuses.

Understand What the Boss Is Saying

You are a leader at some level in the organization or you are an aspiring leader. Your boss is your boss because she or he possesses a combination of leadership competencies that include somewhat effective interpersonal skills (the higher up she or he is, the more likely she or he is to be skilled interpersonally). Your boss has developed sophisticated communication skills. Sometimes bosses are vague, sometimes bosses are indirect, and sometimes they expect you to "fill in the blanks." Whatever your situation, you must develop the skills to understand boss language. In order for you to be competent, you must not only understand what the boss is saying and what he wants, you must act on it.

CONCLUSION

Beyond possessing basic leadership skills, the power of competence means developing the ability to do whatever it takes to get the job done as long as your actions are not unethical, illegal, or immoral. This idea means that competence is a "moving target" based on the particular leadership challenge of the moment and your current boss. What one boss may consider competent performance may require one skill set, and what another boss may consider competent performance may require a different skill set. Don't assume that the leadership competencies that helped you attain a position will help you keep the position. Your solution to ongoing competence is becoming a self-aware, perpetual learner. Try your best to turn every leadership challenge into a learning laboratory. Seek out and respond to feedback. Analyze organizational events, and at the same time develop a deep understanding of what caused the event to happen. If "feedback is the breakfast of champions," then reflection is the bowl in which we place it. Whatever your level of competence, strive to be a developing leader who recognizes and cultivates the power of competence.

ENGAGING SELF AND OTHERS

The following activities and materials are designed to involve you, the reader, and others, as you and they create learning communities. Because our major emphasis in this book is on leadership lessons for adults, the exercises focus on adult learning.

Activity 4.1

Identify the one leadership trait/characteristic where you feel least competent. Explain how you will handle this deficiency. Would you seek additional training, delegate responsibilities, or just "live with the deficiency"? Give the rationale behind your corrective strategy.

_____

_____

_____

_____

Activity 4.2
Understanding and Identifying Barriers
to the Power of Competence

The items below contain factors that may impede effective leadership and the use of the power of competence. Reflect on each of these factors and identify which items may represent barriers to the use of the power of competence. Place a check mark by those that may inhibit your success and analyze them for trends. Take charge of your own learning and address your priority developmental needs.

- ❑ I am aware of weaknesses that, if addressed, would make me more effective, but I haven't done anything about them.
- ❑ I frequently operate on "automatic pilot" without taking the time to learn from experiences.
- ❑ I fail to look beyond the immediate leadership challenge and, therefore, have little understanding of the real cause.
- ❑ I have developed leadership strategies that usually work for me; even when they don't, I keep trying to use the same strategies.
- ❑ I sometimes let my emotions get the best of me, especially in the "heat of battle."
- ❑ I frequently irritate others with my leadership style and actions.
- ❑ I spend too much time analyzing a challenge and not enough time actually doing something about it.
- ❑ I spend too much time analyzing a challenge and fail to seek enough input from others who may have some expertise in the matter.
- ❑ I sometimes see too much or too little "sameness" in leadership challenges.

❑ I am not good at rehearsing possible outcomes that will result from my actions.

❑ I sometimes fail to seek feedback, but if I do I might not act on the feedback.

❑ I sometimes consult with the "wrong" people in seeking assistance with a leadership challenge.

❑ I sometimes will choose to avoid certain types of leadership challenges.

❑ I sometimes fail to get in touch with my true feelings about a situation and, therefore, can't admit to others my true feelings.

❑ I fail to take into consideration the value system of others involved in the situation and, therefore, am really not in touch with how they might be feeling.

❑ I overreact more frequently than I should.

COMPLEMENTARY COMMENTARY

Research for an earlier book, *Staying on Track: An Educational Leader's Guide to Preventing Derailment and Ensuring Personal and Organizational Success* (Corwin Press, 1997), focused on major reasons why leaders derailed. Respondents listed incompetence more than any other factor. Incompetence was defined succinctly as "not equipped to carry out major role functions." Examples of incompetence were indecisiveness, a lack of organizational skills (particularly a lack of follow-through on the leader's rhetoric), and poor "table manners of leadership." By "table manners of leadership," respondents meant that the leader had problems with interpersonal relationships—particularly those small behaviors that facilitate an exchange of information and feelings.

Conversation with a friend in the hotel business brought our attention to the importance of entrance and exit rituals. He had recently read a book on hotel management that argued that a happy guest is one whose first and last impressions are given proper attention. [See S. Kleinfield. *The Hotel* (1989). New York: Simon & Schuster, p. 36.]

Activity 4.3a
Entrance and Exit Rituals

Identify and describe a situation in which proper attention was given to you as you *entered* an organizational setting for the first time.

_____

_____

_____

Leadership Seminar Participant Responses:

> Eye contact communicated an interest in me as a person, and it indicated a willingness to go out of their way and risk a certain kind of vulnerability.

> Smiles and other nonverbal behaviors relaxed me, and we established a connection through what some would call "small talk."

> When I called on the phone, I was greeted with "Good morning. Thank you for calling. How may I help you?"

> I was surprised by the CEO's energy level. It was enough to demonstrate his interest in seeing me, but not so much that it overwhelmed me. He came across as authentic.

> Distractions were removed. I felt like I had her undivided attention. In fact, she asked if it was acceptable for her to take notes. I felt flattered that she would care enough to write down some of the things I had to say.

> With one sentence, the superintendent of schools shared a clear, concise vision: "Everything we do here is aimed at helping children and adults become the best they can be."

Activity 4.3b

Identify and describe a situation where the leader exhibited excellent exit rituals—behaviors that sent you on your way with a good feeling about the leader and the organization.

_____

_____

_____

Leadership Seminar Participant Responses:

> I was happily surprised to discover that she didn't constantly look at her watch or over my shoulder to see if someone else was more deserving of her attention.

> At the end of conversation, he summarized what had taken place in our conversation, thanked me for interest in the organization, and invited me back if the need arose.

> I brought a problem to the table and it was fixed. I will never forget this.

> After our conversation, I was reminded that he called me by name several times and with special emphasis as he walked me to the door.

> She continued our conversation by walking me to my car just outside the building.

COMPLEMENTARY COMMENTARY

Listening is probably the most powerful civility available to you as an effective leader. It is flattering to the speaker, and it demonstrates that you aren't self-centered but instead are eager to learn more about the person speaking. By focusing on the speaker, you will also lessen your anxiety. By actively listening, you will communicate that you understand where the speaker is coming from and care enough about that person to step into his or her shoes. Truly listening to a person will communicate trust and caring—the result often being that the speaker will feel less threatened or less vulnerable and therefore will probably tell you more than originally intended.

Activity 4.4
Listening

Describe a situation where a person in your organization truly listened to you. What were some of the thoughts and feelings you had during this experience?

_____

_____

_____

_____

_____

_____

Leadership Seminar Participant Responses:

I felt truly accepted and not judged for what I said.

I didn't expect the governor to be as attentive as he was. With his busy schedule, he could have treated me as simply a number, but he didn't.

She acted as if she was hearing what I had to say for the first time. It gave me the feeling that she was curious and interested in learning about my opinions.

COMPLEMENTARY COMMENTARY

A communications expert reminded us that "the way we interact with other people—both personally and professionally—has little to do with the written word. It is almost totally based on speaking." [See S. Linver (1978). *Speakeasy.* New York: Summit, p. 18.]

How Good (and Comfortable) Are You as a Public Speaker?

Are you more comfortable relating to people in formal or informal settings? If your style is more formal, use a lectern and stick rather closely to your detailed notes or written speech. If your style is more informal, push the lectern aside and move into the audience as if you were having a conversation. The secret is to share your authentic self with the audience. It is also helpful to focus on the audience rather than yourself. One way to ease your tension is to think about how curious you are to learn more about the audience and their reaction to your ideas. Your desire to connect with the audience will give you energy. Sharing warmth and sense of humor will make a difference in your presentation of self.

The physical setting in which you speak sets the stage for your speaking. In both formal and informal settings, it can be useful to have a mental checklist. For example, remove distractions, such as a gurgling coffeepot; have chairs and/or tables arranged the way you want them; assess acoustics and check equipment; and have a prepared introduction for the person who is introducing you. Your preparation for the situation sends the message, "I care enough about you, the audience, to have done my homework." And good preparation also gives you, the speaker, a sense of security.

You will naturally be nervous to some extent before speaking in many situations. Treat this nervousness as a good thing, for it means that you cared enough about the audience and yourself to get psyched up for the occasion. Self-talk can be helpful as you prepare: "Good going. I have an edge on, and I know that this is necessary in order to do a good job." It is especially helpful to you to realize that the audience wants you to succeed and is, therefore, with you from the start.

One of the advantages speaking has over writing is that you get immediate reaction to your ideas. Because much of your communication is nonverbal body language, you will be able to read your audience and know how your ideas are being received. As you share your warmth with the audience, they will share their warmth with you.

Because more and more leaders are expected to go on television, we have prepared a list of guidelines for this challenge.

Guidelines for Television Speaking

- Talk to the reporter, not the camera or microphone, and look the reporter straight in the eye.
- Stand or sit erectly. Don't stoop or bend over.
- If you say "No comment," add that you will get back to the reporter by such-and-such a time.
- Know who you're dealing with and develop rapport with the reporter when possible.
- Remember that the good photographer (camera person) doesn't always have the camera to his or her eye. The camera can be rolling from any position, even if it is under his or her arm.
- Be politely on your guard all the time.
- Take advantage of nonconfrontational "good news" programs.
- The bottom line is to meet reporters head-on and be honest.
- Be cool and confident. It disarms reporters.
- Remember that our nation has a high degree of sensitivity about minorities and women.
- A smile is the most disarming thing in the world. Bring to the camera the real person inside you.
- Be prepared. If you don't know, say "I don't know."
- There is no such thing as "off the record." Beware of the reporter who says, "This is off the record."
- You can ask to talk to the reporter about something before you go on camera. If the reporter won't allow you to do this, don't talk.
- It is a good idea to suggest a place for the interview. Get an appropriate visual backdrop.
- Watch hazards around you. Don't swivel in a chair. Don't fidget. Calm down, even if it means that you grab a desk in front of you or behind you.
- Take your time.
- Ask to reshoot if you are extremely dissatisfied with the interview.
- Limit the number of remarks and focus on two or three major points.
- Ask the reporter about the people she talked to already, as well as those people she will talk to before the story is over.
- You can occasionally stop a reporter dead in his tracks by saying, "I have no earthly idea what you are talking about."
- Although your organization is on private property, be aware that television cameras can "shoot" onto your property from a nearby site without your permission.

Familiarity with television interviews will be enhanced as you have more and more experience with reporters. How does one get better at this? Winston Churchill was asked what he did in his spare time. He responded, "I rehearse my extemporaneous speeches." [See J. Adams. (1983). *Without Precedent.* New York: Horton, p. 229.]

Activity 4.5
Speaking

This activity will help you assess your comfort and proficiency as a speaker. Think about the items listed and rate your comfort and proficiency on a scale from 1 (low) to 5 (high).

	Comfort	Proficiency
1. Speaking one-to-one.	5 4 3 2 1	5 4 3 2 1
2. Listening one-to-one.	5 4 3 2 1	5 4 3 2 1
3. Answering questions one-to-one.	5 4 3 2 1	5 4 3 2 1
4. Speaking to a small group.	5 4 3 2 1	5 4 3 2 1
5. Listening (as the speaker/leader) and attending to verbal and nonverbal language in a small group.	5 4 3 2 1	5 4 3 2 1
6. Answering questions after speaking to a small group.	5 4 3 2 1	5 4 3 2 1
7. Speaking to a large group.	5 4 3 2 1	5 4 3 2 1
8. Listening (as the speaker/leader) and attending to verbal and nonverbal language in a large group.	5 4 3 2 1	5 4 3 2 1
9. Answering questions after speaking to a large group.	5 4 3 2 1	5 4 3 2 1
10. Telephone interviews.	5 4 3 2 1	5 4 3 2 1
11. Television interviews.	5 4 3 2 1	5 4 3 2 1
12. Radio interviews.	5 4 3 2 1	5 4 3 2 1
13. Newspaper reporter interviews.	5 4 3 2 1	5 4 3 2 1

COMPLEMENTARY COMMENTARY WRITING

Writing affords you with another vehicle for communicating with people interested in your organization. Time and time again, we hear about memos and other literature that have serious spelling and grammatical errors. Correct spelling and grammar are important table manners of leadership. Because we all make spelling and grammatical errors, the secret is to have a proficient copyeditor who will read over your memos and the like. It takes extra effort and time to use a proofreader, but many an embarrassing moment can be avoided with such effort.

We occasionally hear about or see in newspapers stories about how e-mails are inadvertently copied to people who become upset about the sender's message. And we are reminded that organizations consider computers and their content to belong to them rather than the person using the computers.

An important question to ask in sending a letter, memorandum, or e-mail is, "What is my purpose in doing this?" This purpose should be clearly stated, with concrete next steps spelled out concisely and precisely, so that recipients can know what they are expected to do in response to your communication. In the case of letters or other hard-copy materials, if you want to be sure of a response, include a stamped, self-addressed envelope.

Finally, always send clean copy. Badly photocopied materials send the message that you are sloppy and unprofessional.

Miscellaneous Table Manners of Leadership

The following are some miscellaneous table manners that can be very important:

- When leaving a message on a telephone answering machine or voice mail, state your name, telephone number, nature of the business, and the best time to return the call. *State this information slowly.* Remember that the person listening to your request is probably writing down the information.
- Before meeting with other persons or having important phone conversations, prepare for the content of your conversation, even if this means writing notes from which to speak.
- Always give your full name when making a phone call. Many people begin speaking, and the other party has no idea who it is.
- There are two major ways to assure yourself that you can do something with the support of your "bureaucratic superiors": (a) remove irritants; and (b) be willing to share the credit if efforts are successful and share the blame if they are not.
- When substantive agreements are made over the telephone, follow up with a memorandum of understanding (hard copy or e-mail), concluding with, "Unless I hear from you otherwise, I'll assume this is correct."
- Log important contact with other parties. You will need to include the time of the contact, the person contacted, and the substance of the contact.
- A seminar participant added the following to this list: "Choose your battles. Don't sweat the small stuff."

With regard to all of the table manners of leadership discussed in this section of the book, we would do well to remind ourselves that all forms of communication are promissory. We promise that we will act out what we have said we will do. And, keeping our promises, while using the table manners of leadership, demonstrates the power of competence and increases the chances for personal and organizational success.

CASE 4: Relating to Employees Who Fake Competence

A consultant from an outside agency has just completed his assessment of your organization. The consultant sits down with you in your office to review the report. You are impressed with the thoroughness and insightfulness of the consultant's work, but one specific criticism of your organization really gets your attention: "Some of your employees pretend they know things that they really don't know. In short, they fake competencies."
How will you respond to this criticism?

_____

_____

_____

_____

_____

_____

Authors' Recommendations

The first thing you need from the consultant is specific examples of the criticism: "Who are the employees and how are they faking competencies?" You will need to keep in mind that there may be a wide range of fakery. It can run from exaggeration to pathological lying.

The second step is to find out to the best of your ability why this fakery is taking place: "What's in it for the employee to engage in this behavior? Is the organization putting undue pressure on its employees to deliver what is expected? Are the organization's expectations realistic? What do the employees in question have in common? For example, if the employees in question are relatively recent hires, have they had inadequate training for the position they have assumed? Or do these few employees simply have character flaws that have led to this predicament?" You are challenged to look for patterns.

Also, how does it cost both the employee and the organization for such fakery to occur? What are the results of this fakery? Your findings in this regard will be helpful in taking next steps.

It is important to realize that in the process of dealing with the questions above, you will be relating to *all* employees who are privy to formal and informal communication channels. And, the credibility of all employees as well as the organization is at stake.

SELF INVENTORY

Now that you have completed the readings and activities on "The Power of Competence," think about what you've learned and respond to the following items on a five-point scale: 1 (low) to 5 (high).

1. My ability to identify competencies in others.   _____

2. My ability to identify incompetencies in others.   _____

3. My ability to identify competencies in myself.   _____

4. My ability to identify incompetencies in myself.   _____

5. My ability to truly listen to what others are saying.   _____

6. My ability to articulate my ideas one-on-one.   _____

7. My ability to articulate my ideas in a small group setting.   _____

8. My ability to articulate my ideas in a large group setting.   _____

9. If I think I can get away with it, I sometimes fake competencies.   _____

10. I feel adequately prepared to help persons who are accountable to me when they fake competencies.   _____

Note: If you are in a group setting, form discussion groups in order to share and summarize findings.

Scoring for Self Inventory

Total the ratings and find your score in the following scale:

41–50	Superior
31–40	Above Average
21–30	Average
11–20	Below Average
0–10	Poor

SUGGESTED READINGS

Astin, H., & Leland, C. (1991). *Women of Influence, Women of Vision: A Cross-Generational Study of Leaders and Social Change*. San Francisco: Jossey-Bass.

Barth, R. S. (2003). *Lessons Learned: Shaping Relationships and the Culture of the Workplace*. Thousand Oaks, CA: Corwin Press.

Brubaker, D. L., & Coble, L. D. (1997). *Staying on Track: An Educational Leader's Guide to Preventing Derailment and Ensuring Personal and Organizational Success*. Thousand Oaks, CA: Corwin Press.

Sashkin, S., & Sashkin, M. G. (2003). *Leadership That Matters: The Critical Factors for Making a Difference in People's Lives and Organizations' Success*. New York: Berrett-Koehler.

5

The Power of
Wanting to Be There

Dale L. Brubaker

A few years ago, our family went to a favorite restaurant to celebrate our daughter's birthday. We were greeted cordially by the hostess and led to our table. The waitperson approached our table and said, "Can I help you?" in a voice devoid of emotion. She wasn't unpleasant and she wasn't pleasant. She was simply there. Our family reacted to her flattened affect by trying to pick up her spirits with humor and caring comments. No response. The result of this lack of interaction with the waitperson—the leader who was expected to set the stage for a pleasant evening—was that the food was excellent but the total dining experience was not. While riding home in the car, one of our children said, "The waitress acted as if she didn't want to be with us."

This experience caused me to think about the importance of the leader sending a powerful message to others: "I want to be with you." I suspect that each of us enters the work world daily asking the question, "Do my leaders at work think my contribution is special enough to want to be with me?" When the answer is "yes," the day seems to be a little shorter and the quality of one's work is likely to be better.

Teachers probably look to administrators, and children look to teachers, with the same question in mind: "Do you want to be here with me?" When people believe that their leaders want to be with them, it won't necessarily assure successful leadership. If they believe that the leader doesn't want to be with them, however, it certainly works against effective leadership.

The secret to "wanting to be there" is to know that what you are doing is an extension of what you really value. It is presenting your true inner self to others. One of the most famous radio and television newscasters of all time, Edward R. Murrow, openly admitted that he had "mike fright" before each broadcast. It took him a few minutes to get rolling, but then he began to experience the celebration of doing something well. He kept on doing it, and he did well.

Elizabeth Dole's life story is a wonderful demonstration of a person whose remarkable public service career serving five U.S. presidents is an extension of what she really values—the key to "wanting to be there." As a young woman, she left the small town of Salisbury, North Carolina, to attend Duke University, where she graduated with distinction. She earned a law degree, as well as a master's degree in education and government, from Harvard University. She served as Deputy Assistant for Consumer Affairs to President Nixon and was the first female Secretary of Transportation, a cabinet member in the Reagan administration. She was named Secretary of Labor in 1989, in President George H. W. Bush's administration, and left this position in 1991 to become only the second woman since founder Clara Barton to serve as president of the American Red Cross. Later she was elected to the U.S. Senate. A hallmark of Elizabeth Dole's success is her caring for others and her love for her work. Her quiet competence-in-action is a model for others who wish to lead.

FINDING YOUR MOTIVATION

It is a challenge to all of us to break through our initial fears until we reach a comfort level that allows us to be our best. Repeated fulfillment in meeting challenges eventually results in what ballet dancers call "muscular memory," a subconscious process that directs you through the performance of your task even when your mind goes blank.

We can expect this same tension level just before giving a speech, chairing an important meeting, or selling an idea to a new client. Once the performance begins, the leader becomes so involved in the presentation that he or she will simply do what needs to be done. It is only later that many leaders collapse with exhaustion, wondering how they did such a good job. But deep down, they know why: because they were motivated.

With these thoughts in mind, I asked a university sophomore, who happened to be seated next to me on a flight from Greensboro to Boston, "How do you know during the first few minutes of a new class if the professor wants to be with you?" This was her response:

> The first thing I look at is the way the professor walks into the classroom. Is he standoffish or does he look at the students? If he looks at the class, and particularly if he has eye contact with each student, the professor has something at stake.
>
> Then I look to see if he expects us to work. There are several ways this is shown. Does he bring the textbook with him? If he does, this demonstrates the important place the book will have in the course.

If the professor brings in the book, does he place it on the table with respect or does he toss it down as if it's not very important?

I also listen to the firmness of his voice. If his voice is firm, this is a first step in telling us that he has high expectations.

The professor's energy level tells me if he is interested in me. He must have a high energy level to set high expectations, but his being reasonably relaxed tells me he thinks I can meet these expectations.

I can tell almost immediately if the professor expects interaction between himself and the students and among students. Does he expect us to be passive or does he encourage us to ask real questions that don't have easy answers? And, does he listen to our answers or is he so glued to his notes that he isn't interested in learning from us?

I'm really bothered if the professor immediately plays favorites. If he does, he is probably there for social reasons and not for the course itself. He wants our approval.

At the end of the conversation, this bright, articulate university student passionately delivered a postscript:

You need to be aware of something with us. We need guidance, even to be told what to do at times, because we're afraid of failure. The fewer decisions we make, the less risk of failure there is. Some of us are miserable, and we see ourselves as victims because we see others as having so much compared to us. You have a challenge with us: If you can, move us beyond these feelings to accept responsibility.

The conviction in the student's answer to my initial question said a great deal. She shared the simple but powerful truth that our enthusiasm for our work keeps us from becoming cynical—the deadliest of leadership qualities. A 19-year-old reminded me that, as leaders in business, industry, education, and other organizations, we have at our fingertips an obvious and often overlooked source of power—wanting to be there.

Implications for Leaders

Larry D. Coble

ORIENTATION

The power of wanting to be there, in a leadership role, is twofold; you must certainly want to be there, but your reasons for wanting to be there must be grounded in a desire to lead the continuous improvement of your organization.

Over my career, I have witnessed and worked with many leaders who want to be in a leadership position, but they want to be there because of a power trip, the trappings of the executive office, or some other reason that is ego-centered as opposed to making the organization a better performing organization.

Executive leadership roles and individuals who possess a strong desire to be there are made for each other. Typically, executive leadership requires long hours, time away from family, and difficulty in having one's own needs for physical exercise and recreation deferred to the interests of the organization and the needs of the individuals in the organization. Time and energy are finite. As a leader, you will experience time limitations and energy limitations. You can give 100 percent, but that is all you can give. Your 100 percent in all likelihood will be working a minimum of ten-hour days, and, more likely, twelve- to fourteen-hour days will frequently dominate your lifestyle. To become highly effective, you must seek out high-leverage activities, activities that produce the greatest return on your investment of time and energy. In my experience, however, few shortcuts produce more time for you away from the job.

WANTING TO BE THERE VERSUS UPWARD MOBILITY

Leaders who want to be there have a strong desire to lead as well as a propensity for risk taking and a high need to achieve. The power of wanting to be there means not only doing a good job with tough challenges, but also having a desire to master the challenge. In other words, doing a good job is not enough; it's wanting to perform at exceptionally high levels as a leader that tends to demonstrate to yourself and others that you want to be there. A word of caution: don't become overly ambitious at the expense of others in your organization. If your peers, your direct reports, or your boss begin to believe that you are a "get ahead at all cost" kind of leader, you will quickly find that you will begin to lose the support of those people whose support is absolutely imperative if you are to become successful. Don't confuse wanting to be there with wanting to get ahead at whatever the human cost to others.

THE IMPORTANCE OF RELATIONSHIPS

Leaders who really want to be there make having relationships with others the most important aspect of their job. They realize that they can't accomplish very much alone and that their success, in large measure, depends on the quality of the relationships that they are able to develop with their co-workers. These relationships will cause such outcomes as having others want to commit to the goals of the organization, demonstrate general buy-in, and want to follow the leader.

You can demonstrate for yourself and others the power of wanting to be there if you are sincere in your desire to send personal, handwritten congratulatory notes to your co-workers, especially your subordinates. From time to time, I will run into former employees in restaurants and airports and, on several occasions, I have had employees mention a handwritten note that I had sent fifteen or twenty years ago that had meant so much to them. Many of these employees frequently mention that they have kept the notes over the years. A congratulatory e-mail is okay, but it will not produce the results that a handwritten note from the boss will produce.

Get out of your office and meet and greet people. Make frequent visits to the "shop floor." See your people face to face. Shake hands with your people. Take whatever steps are appropriate to enable others to feel comfortable around you. Think about your body language and the way you enter and exit the room. Don't be afraid to have appropriate physical contact. A touch on the back or arm demonstrates that you are human and that you want the people in your organization to see you as being human. This may sound strange to the reader, but people in organizations tend to create personalities for their leaders. If they don't know you, then they fill in the blanks.

Demonstrate sincere concern for the welfare of others. Taking the time to mingle with those with whom you work not only indicates that you care, it affords you the opportunity to learn as well. When you are with your co-workers, whether they are peers, bosses, or direct reports, be conscious of what others are thinking, feeling, and doing. Learn from what you observe. To the extent possible, become aware of their roles and responsibilities. Share in their good fortunes and difficult times. Celebrate their successes and empathize with their problems. Be open and accessible. Let others know who you are and what you stand for. And do all of this for the right reason, the reason that you want to be there with them. If you are perceived as a leader who sincerely wants to be there, the people in your organization who serve under your leadership will do what's right because they will trust in you and your motives.

CHANGE

If you are a leader who wants to be there, you will be preoccupied with making your organization a higher performing organization. This means that some of the processes and procedures that are in place will need to be adjusted or "tweaked," and some may require radical surgery. Some earlier innovations will be preserved, some eliminated, and some new ones implemented. Your leadership role includes preserving the best of the past while leading a change effort to the future. Use evaluation methods and other forms of feedback to develop a deep understanding of the organization's performance, but do this in the context of respecting the culture that is in place when you arrive.

Remember that change happens first to individuals and then to the organization. Demonstrate, through your emotional commitment, your support for the best of the existing culture. Become the head cheerleader. Lead others to want to be involved, and solicit their assistance in helping to distinguish between what is significant and what is less important. You should be the first to accept the responsibility for failures and deficiencies in the organization. Demonstrate that you are enthusiastic about all aspects of your job.

Build a higher performing organization through creative construction and eliminate negative, unproductive practices. Become a bureaucracy "buster." Ask your subordinates and other co-workers such questions as these: How might I be of service to you? What do you need from me to enable you to do your job more effectively? What kind of resources do you need that are not currently available to you?

LIFE BALANCE

If you are reading this book, there is a very good chance that you are already in a leadership role or aspiring to one. There is also a very good chance that, if you have your ego under reasonable control, you want to lead for the right reasons. If all of this is true, I would bet that your life is already somewhat out of balance. I can promise you that as you have increases in responsibility and visibility, to perform effectively, your life will become even more out of balance. It is highly probable that as long as you lead, and you lead because of who you are, the best that you can hope for is to be *less unbalanced*. Your need to achieve, to master challenges, and to lead will always represent barriers to a balanced life style.

To lead effectively, you must want to be there, but *don't always be there*. Take the time to enjoy your family and to participate in spiritual development, recreational activities, and an overall wellness program. You may find that you have to approach this "forced" balancing act the same way you would other leadership challenges. To do this, you may have to *schedule* these activities. You may need to employ extremely creative ways of addressing these important aspects of your life. Do whatever it takes, but make it work for you.

CONCLUSION

Leading effectively means wanting to be there to lead. Leaders who recognize the power of wanting to be there value the contributions of all stakeholders, including those who are often overlooked or whose views are frequently dismissed by the majority. Leaders who want to be there are open to new ideas, strive to eliminate internal competition among their colleagues, and demonstrate ethical behavior as a core value. Leaders who want to be there ask the right questions and help others ask the right questions. Wanting to be there involves personal integrity and means becoming an outstanding listener, teacher, and one who is committed to the development of followers and the improvement of the organization.

ENGAGING SELF AND OTHERS

The following activities and materials are designed to involve you, the reader, and others, as you and they create learning communities. Because our major emphasis in this book is on leadership lessons for adults, the exercises focus on adult learning.

Activity 5.1

Over the past five years, you have worked on your job for an average of 11 hours per day. During your last visit to your family doctor, she told you to reduce the hours spent working each day to 8 or 9. You are committed to following your doctor's advice.

What strategies will you employ and/or what activities will you give up to reduce your work hours? Discuss the rationale behind your decision.

_____

_____

_____

_____

_____

Activity 5.2

Since arriving at your new leadership job, you have made it a practice to visit each work station in your building for 5 to 10 minutes each month, at which time you discuss problems or just pass the time of day. Recently, your Board of Directors has recommended that you curtail or eliminate this practice. You are required to respond to their recommendation. What will you say?

_____

_____

_____

_____

_____

Activity 5.3

Recently you have become more and more bored with your leadership role. What steps can you take to re-create the enthusiasm you once had for your job?

_____

_____

_____

_____

_____

Activity 5.4
Am I There?

Read each of the following behaviors and place a check mark next to those you frequently use or that apply to you.

Am I There Checklist

- ❏ I love the work I do.
- ❏ I emphasize the human aspects of my job as well as the techniques and procedures.
- ❏ I demonstrate that I am enthusiastic about my role in the organization.
- ❏ I become involved with the personnel in my organization.
- ❏ I understand how employees view their roles in the organization.
- ❏ I develop a good balance between work and my personal life.
- ❏ I share the successes and misfortunes of my subordinates.
- ❏ I regularly assess what is going on in the organization.
- ❏ I make a concentrated effort to encourage staff to support the mission of the organization.
- ❏ I visit work sites to learn about and support staff members.
- ❏ I take responsibility for failures in the organization and make efforts to correct deficiencies.

COMPLEMENTARY COMMENTARY

Leadership seminar participants who are introduced to *the power of wanting to be there* share an abundance of stories on this subject. These participants say they know, within the first few minutes of a seminar presenter's introduction, whether or not he or she wants to be there. A sample of remarks follows:

> "It was obvious from the physical setup of the room that we were in that attention was given to this matter."

> "The energy level of the speaker got our attention."

> "The handouts demonstrated that the speaker did her homework."

> "He greeted each of us as we came into the room, had a firm handshake, and looked us in the eye."

Activity 5.5

Identify and describe a situation or setting in which you knew that a leader *wanted* to be with you.

_____

_____

_____

_____

Now, identify and describe a situation or setting in which you knew that the leader *did not want* to be with you.

_____

_____

_____

_____

_____

Leadership Seminar Participant Responses:

WANTED TO BE THERE	DID NOT WANT TO BE THERE
Connected with us with warm greeting (verbal, nonverbal, physical bearing invited me to the setting).	Distanced self from us (flattened affect and literally kept his distance).
Energy left us with the feeling that she cared about us and the subject matter.	Relatively passive—little energy, seemed distracted.
Sense of humor appropriate for occasion—sense of playfulness and creativity conveyed.	No sense of humor and occasionally seemed jaded and cynical.
Had an agenda that demonstrated organization of ideas, but also willing to leave agenda for important side-issues.	Didn't stray from the agenda—seemed simply to want to cover agenda.
	No agenda—"loosey, goosey."

Activity 5.6a

The leader who feels that he or she has something to offer others has a healthy self-concept: "I can make a difference!"

What is it that motivates such a leader? Seminar participants find it helpful to reach back into their childhood pasts in order to answer this question.

Think for a few minutes of those times when you were a child and had a sense of awe, wonder, and amazement. Describe a few experiences you had as a child during which your curiosity and sense of exploration drove you forward and led to new understandings.

_____

_____

_____

_____

_____

Leadership Seminar Participant Responses:

> When I was 7 or 8 my dad let me use his bamboo fishing pole. I could fish for myself. I caught and ate 17 bluegills. The bobber kept going under. My brothers couldn't believe their sister caught all of these fish. Everybody said, "How wonderful!"

> I rode a train as a second grader. I had life space away from my family.

> The first time I snorkeled I was 5 years old. The bluefish kept touching me.

> I remember the first day of school—the sounds, smells, colors. The room was clean and neat.

> I'll never forget the first day I learned to drive in the driveway. I was 13.

> I remember listening to my cousin being born. I was 6 and stood outside and beneath the window. I saw my aunt with the baby on her lap. My aunt had a flat stomach again.

> I rode an escalator in Birmingham when I was 12. We only had a one-story house in Enterprise, Alabama, and so this was a totally different experience for me.

> I felt the warmth and saw the glow of the volcano 30 miles away. Where did everything go? I wondered. . . .

Activity 5.6b

Return now to your present position in the organization where you work. Briefly describe a few experiences you have had when you sensed the same kind of awe, wonder, and amazement you experienced on occasion as a child.

Now that you have described these experiences, what characteristics do they have in common with the experiences you described from childhood?

_____

_____

_____

_____

_____

Leadership Seminar Participant Responses:

A sense of playfulness and even a kind of humor.

Risk taking; breaking routine, tradition, and ritual.

A caring attitude toward others, the challenges, and self.

A sense of my inner strength that comes from courage, commitment, and conviction.

The feeling of being totally absorbed—where I didn't notice the time.

A sensitive attitude that allowed me to sense, in depth, what I was focusing on.

The desire to do whatever I was doing well.

The pure delight that comes from meeting the challenge.

CASE 5: The Challenge in Motivating Oneself and Others

After attending a leadership seminar on leadership and motivation, you have an increased awareness of the importance of this subject. You notice that apathy seems to "swim" through some parts of your organization, whereas other parts are full of life. The difference seems to come down to whether or not members of the organization want to come to work. This is obvious in their verbal and nonverbal ways of communicating with each other.

You feel challenged to give attention to this matter systematically, and you also realize that motivation is an issue that must be constantly attended to rather than being introduced and then dropped. How will you meet this challenge, given your position as a recognized leader responsible for morale in your organization?

_____

_____

_____

_____

_____

_____

Authors' Recommendations

The motivation problem in your organization has no quick fix. Therefore, you must realize that dramatic, short-term measures, such as bringing in a well-known motivational speaker, are of limited value.

A good place to start is by listing the basic assumptions you hold with regard to effective leadership. For example, the leader at the top of an organization, or formally assigned to head a part of your organization, sets the tone and therefore must be assessed with regard to behaviors that foster and/or inhibit people having a positive attitude toward work and colleagues. Another example of a basic assumption is the view that for some things to change, other things must remain the same.

After you have listed your basic assumptions with regard to effective leadership, how are these operational guidelines being practiced in the organization as a whole, as well as the particular parts of the organization? You may wish to target a part of the organization initially as a kind of pilot system for assessing morale.

Once you have done the kind of pre-assessment that yields valuable information, you are ready to consider strategies for changing some things and conserving others. You will obviously be challenged to convince members of the organization as a whole and/or members of a part of the organization to buy into and own strategies employed.

It is especially important that you recognize that your own attitudes and behavior will be a model for others in the organization. Your energy, intelligence, and desire to be a team player who cares about others and the organization will be tested each step of the way. You will need a core group of colleagues who will guide and support your efforts.

SELF INVENTORY

Now that you have completed the readings and activities on "The Power of Wanting to Be There," think about what you've learned and respond to the following items on a five-point scale: 1 (low) to 5 (high).

1. My desire to be in my present organization. _____

2. My desire to be in the position I hold in this organization. _____

3. My ability to identify the ways in which I communicate my desire to be in a leadership position. _____

4. My ability to identify the ways in which other leaders communicate their desire to be in a leadership position. _____

5. My proficiency in having direct eye-contact with others. _____

6. My proficiency in private one-on-one discourse. _____

7. My proficiency in public discourse. _____

8. My willingness to break through my fears to do something I need to do in order to be an effective leader. _____

9. My ability to present my true inner self to others. _____

10. My ability to generate enthusiasm as an antidote to cynicism. _____

Note: If you are in a group setting, form discussion groups in order to share and summarize findings.

Scoring for Self Inventory
    Total the ratings and find your score in the following scale:

41–50	Superior
31–40	Above Average
21–30	Average
11–20	Below Average
0–10	Poor

SUGGESTED READINGS

Bennis, W. (2003). *On Becoming a Leader*. New York: Addison-Wesley.

Dole, E., & Dole, B., with Smith, R. N., & Tymchuk, K. (1996). *Unlimited Partners: Our American Story*. New York: Simon & Schuster.

MacNeil, R. (2003). *Looking for My Country: Finding Myself in America*. New York: Random House.

Nee-Benham, A. N., & Cooper, J. (1998). *Let My Spirit Soar: Narratives of Diverse Women in School Leadership*. Thousand Oaks, CA: Corwin Press.

Neumann, A., & Peterson, P. (1997). *Learning From Our Lives: Women, Research, and Autobiography in Education*. New York: Teachers College Press.

6

The Power of Passion

Dale L. Brubaker

George Uhlig, co-founder of the United States Sports Academy, was raised in an area of Nebraska that he describes as "so rural that we came toward town to hunt." Furthermore, every boy not on his death bed was expected to play baseball.

Uhlig's ability to manage was tapped during his senior year in high school. His baseball coach left to work in the defense industry, and George became a coach as well as a player. He learned to deal with a challenge faced by all leaders in business and government. He was the first among equals, a member of the team, and the designated leader of the team.

Uhlig found himself energized by this leadership challenge. As he told me once, "I like to organize things. I like to make things work. I learned as a coach that you work with—not against—people."

After graduating from high school in the early 1950s, Uhlig spent four years at the University of Nebraska, where he was on the baseball team. Upon graduation, his coach wrote: "Mr. Uhlig has never played an inning, but yet is the most loyal and one of the hardest workers I have ever had. Although lacking in physical ability, I would highly recommend him as a coach. He will be a great influence on young people."

Can you imagine being a member of a baseball team for four years and not playing an inning? How did Uhlig react? He recognized that his teammates, most of whom were Korean War veterans, were better than he was, and he used his strong desire and work ethic to help the team during practice sessions. He also used his position as a member of the team to practice his organizational skills.

One of the main problems Uhlig learned to deal with was tension between the individual and the group . . . tension that must be reconciled for both to excel. "Baseball is a unique sport," according to Uhlig. "Think about it! It's played in a team environment, but is really a combination of a subset of collaborations. The pitcher and catcher. The second base combination on the double play and steal. But, by and large, it's an individual effort. The batter versus the ball. The pitcher versus the bat. The infielder versus the grounder."

Although George Uhlig didn't become a famous baseball player, his comments demonstrate a leadership quality that is a tremendous source of power—*passion for an activity or enterprise.*

Uhlig gave his heart and soul to improving his high school and university baseball teams—a commitment to sports leadership that continues to this day. He lived the dictionary's definition of passion: "a strong fondness and enthusiasm of a powerful and compelling nature."

WHAT CREATES THIS PASSION WITHIN US?

A series of events that calls us into action will often release our passion. This was the case with George Uhlig. He appraised his own talents as a baseball player and manager honestly in order to help the team. He knew that, compared to other seasoned veterans, he was somewhat wanting as a first-stringer, but, at the same time, he recognized the key role he could play in training and managing the team. He could have quit or simply gone through the motions. Instead, he focused on his strengths and starved his weaknesses. He made a difference!

A passion within us is often stimulated by an unplanned critical incident— an event marked by pain and sorrow. These experiences force us out of our comfort zone.

The news media contain stories about famous people who lose children or who experience broken relationships, after which passion for a related cause is released. Actor Carroll O'Conner's anti-drug campaign following the drug-related death of his son is an example. He used his new-found passion for a good cause to turn a "breakdown" into a "breakthrough."

After a few depressing months in New York City at the beginning of his career, comedian Robin Williams said, "Once in a while, it's good to have a nervous breakdown. A little emotional house cleaning never hurt anybody."[1]

It's interesting that the word "passion" comes from the Latin word *passionem,* meaning suffering. Hence, we're reminded of the famous medieval passion play staged every ten years in Oberammergau, Germany—a play that centers its attention on the sufferings of Jesus Christ.

THE BENEFITS OF A LEADER'S PASSION

The advantages of a leader's passion for an activity or enterprise are many and diverse. Arthur M. Schlesinger Jr., adviser to President Kennedy and author of

A Life in the Twentieth Century, described passion as "the marvelous quality of intensifying life so that others feel that they have perceived more and thought more and understood more."[2]

Passion can help you set aside or work through fears and anxieties associated with what you are doing and, in the process, gain confidence.

Katharine Graham's 1997 book, *Personal History,* is a candid account of a courageous leader who used her passion to overcome self-doubt that stemmed from a number of origins, including a self-absorbed mother and a dynamic husband who discounted her talents as a leader. When Phil Graham took his own life in 1963, she stepped into the leadership void at the *Washington Post* and won the support of her employees with a combination of dedication, hard work, and a desire to learn the newspaper business. Her book won a Pulitzer Prize, and she was internationally recognized as one of the last great newspaper owner-publishers.

Passion can focus your attention so that you aren't distracted by less important matters. It must be consistent, persistent, and disciplined in order to avoid fickleness and faddism. The passionate leader is often a "nudger" who keeps others and him- or herself on track.

Because passion is driven by curiosity, it often leads to new discoveries and keeps your ego in check. The leader who is a good listener and conversationalist communicates love for the task at hand in order to realize organizational and personal vision. Love for the activity or enterprise is contagious and combats clock watching. Top-down hierarchies designed to control people are beside the point, and ownership, not imitation, is the norm.

Leaders who feel a passion for their work often turn the mundane into something more. Upon Katharine Graham's death in 2001, the famous and not-so-famous recalled her simple kindnesses—notes, phone calls, and comments of concern about difficulties that others and their children experienced.

In conclusion, passion is pivotal. It's a necessary condition for creative leadership. The important role that passion can play makes it clear that creative leadership is much more than a list of technical skills. Attitudes and understandings are at the heart of meeting the leadership challenge in any aspect of life. And the driving force for such attitudes and understandings is one's passion.

Implications for Leaders

Larry D. Coble

ORIENTATION

Basic to the leadership process is having a leader who is passionate about his or her work. A leader who understands the power of passion is a leader who loves the work he or she does. The thing about passion is that it is not a generic trait that is present with every leader in every situation. Passion goes with a particular challenge that may be within the realm of a general career choice, or it may be more directly aligned with a challenge or a specific assignment within a particular vocation or profession. An example might be an employee who works at NASA and enjoys his work, but who becomes passionate about a new assignment as lead technician on the next shuttle launch.

GENETIC PREDISPOSITION AND EARLY DEVELOPMENTAL EXPERIENCES

The experiences that seem to be most significant in shaping the power of passion are those that leaders have experienced in early childhood. These passion-producing experiences tend to be those during which the leader, as a child, found unusual success or unusual pain. With my own early experiences, I quickly developed a passion for the game of baseball, because playing the game offered me an opportunity for recognition that helped enhance my sense of self-worth and my self-esteem. This passion for excelling in baseball was closely related to my second passion, which was to overcome growing up in poverty during my early years. I desperately wanted to achieve what would have been considered middle-class social status. I was literally *driven* to do what I had to do to escape the embarrassment that went with being less well-off financially than the rest of my friends and most of my classmates. These passions translated into a high need to achieve, both in athletic competition and in the classroom.

I therefore developed one passion fueled by success on the baseball field and one passion fueled by the pain and embarrassment of living in poverty. Absent my successes in athletics and in the classroom, I would never have developed the confidence in myself to achieve and ultimately rise to the top of numerous organizations.

PAIN AND PASSION

Painful experiences, sometimes translated and internalized as failures, seem to be at the very core of one's development as a leader. The list is almost endless when you take into account leaders whose early childhood beginnings were less than positive and who, as a result of these beginnings, became driven to succeed.

It is extremely important to note that not every leader can have a childhood that begins in poverty or other extreme circumstances that tend to ignite their drive for success. What developing leaders must realize, however, is that unless you experience some pain and possible failure, you are going to miss an essential understanding that effective leaders value. If pain and failure are missing from your early childhood experiences, it is imperative that they be present somewhere along the way to the executive suite. Be thankful for those incompetent bosses, challenging assignments that are nearly impossible to complete, and anything and everything else that causes you discomfort and an opportunity to stretch. These experiences build the foundation for your effectiveness.

PERSONAL AND ORGANIZATIONAL SUCCESSES

The power of passion can almost guarantee personal and organizational success, or passion misused can guarantee personal and organizational failure. Highly effective leaders develop a deep and unapologetic understanding of their true passions. They also recognize that that their passions can be so powerful that they can interfere with sound reasoning and judgment. We can readily see the power of passion when used positively as a rallying point for renewed pride in America following the dark days of September 11, 2001. We can also see the evil face of misused passion in our enemies who detest America and Americans.

As a leader, you must never use your passion in a destructive manner, and you must always recognize that your passion can be directed at bringing about both good and evil. When positive passion is coupled with knowledge and skill, individual and organizational performance increase significantly, and routine activities become enjoyable adventures.

PASSION AND PERSONNEL

One of the basic traits that should be considered in employing new personnel is whether or not the employees demonstrate a potential for having the passion to do the job under consideration. Having co-workers and direct reports who approach their responsibilities with devotion and passion makes the leader's life easier. The best way to ensure that this is the case is to make sure that the "right stuff" is present on the front end, at the hiring process. Developing the ability as a leader to identify passion in your employees will go a long way in helping you determine the difference in a good employee and a potentially outstanding employee. People with true passion continuously raise their achievement bar. Those who fail to raise the bar will see the passion that was present begin to fade.

CONCLUSION

Recognizing the power of passion is also recognizing the power that resides within the heart and soul of the leader and other high-achieving, driven individuals. Passion used constructively results in high-performing individuals and high-performing organizations that focus on high-quality outcomes in both relationships and the bottom line. Passion used inappropriately results in destructive outcomes for all involved. Strive to be a leader who understands your true passion and then channels that true passion in a direction of positive leadership. Show me a highly successful individual, and I will show you a person who is endowed with passion.

ENGAGING SELF AND OTHERS

The following activities and materials are designed to involve you, the reader, and others, as you and they create learning communities. Because our major emphasis in this book is on leadership lessons for adults, the exercises focus on adult learning.

Activity 6.1

A couple of members of your leadership team appear to be losing their passion to help achieve the mission and goals of your organizations. As a leader, what are the steps that you would use to re-create "fire in their bellies"?

_____

_____

_____

_____

_____

Activity 6.2

Reflect on your past experiences and list five ways/strategies that can be employed to develop passion for the organization on the part of yourself and your employees. Should threat be employed as a legitimate strategy?

_____

_____

_____

_____

_____

Activity 6.3

Place a check mark next to each of the principles/behaviors that you have applied in your professional life.

- ❏ I am aware that passion can be employed to bring about most positive and negative results.
- ❏ I believe that passion for a principle or a job can significantly increase performance and behavior.
- ❏ I encourage my staff to approach their responsibilities with passion and devotion.
- ❏ I believe that people who are endowed with passion continuously raise their performance bar.
- ❏ I believe that passion can be directed at bringing about both good and bad results.
- ❏ I am aware that tragedies and failures often create passion to put forth even more effort.
- ❏ I believe that most successful people have a deep passion for doing well in their jobs.
- ❏ I believe that passion can be so strong that it frequently interferes with sound judgments.

Activity 6.4

Identify and describe an event, project, or challenge for which you have had a passion during your career.

_____

_____

_____

_____

As you look at this description, what characterizes this experience? In other words, what created this passion within you? And what were the benefits of your passion for this event, project, or challenge?

_____

_____

_____

_____

Leadership Seminar Participant Responses:

I didn't seek out or plan for the challenge that presented itself; when it occurred, I wasn't sure I was up to the task. A colleague who had written the grant proposal resigned, and I was asked to take her place as project head when the grant proposal was funded. Now that we are a year into implementing the project, I feel more comfortable, and my passion for the project and work itself has given me understandings and meaning.

The opportunity to teach a course as an adjunct professor at the university was something that I had never considered. To be honest, I never thought of myself in this role. But once I got through my initial nervousness, I discovered that in teaching masters' students I was motivated to learn more about the subject I taught and, as a result, I had more enthusiasm for my work. I began to make connections between my work world and my teaching world.

If anyone had told me a year or so ago that I would become involved in the community's mental health organization, I would have been shocked. However, my child's diagnosis as bipolar opened up an entirely new world to our family. Our lives have changed—for the better in many respects, although it has not been easy.

When members of the seminar discussed the *characteristics* of their stories, they arrived at the following conclusions:

- The event that triggered their passion for a project or challenge was unplanned.
- The unplanned event brought new life to their personal and professional lives.
- The passion they felt took them through their initial anxieties in taking on the challenges they faced.
- Successfully meeting the challenges gave them new understandings and confidence.
- Simply staying in one's comfort zone and not taking on new challenges can lead to boredom and even cynicism.
- A passion for something does not mean that life is problem free. In fact, it is in working through the pain and problems that we have learned the most.

Activity 6.5

Seminar participants were especially intrigued by Arthur M. Schlesinger Jr.'s view that passion has "the marvelous quality of intensifying life." Members of the seminar were challenged by the idea that it is important to share this passion and intensification of life with other colleagues in the organization, as well as with others outside of the organization.

What are some ways that you believe this can be done?

_____

_____

_____

Leadership Seminar Participant Responses:

> Our own enthusiasm and sharing of our passion with others one on one is probably the best vehicle for influencing others.

> Print and nonprint media can be powerful. Newsletters that include our own stories can be very effective.

> Speaking at conferences, conventions, civic organization meetings, and the like can reach people.

> Listening to other people's stories, especially of challenges in their lives, can provide the opening for telling our stories and connecting them with the lives of others.

> We can use the rituals of our organizations to celebrate our passions.

> Our organization should find ways to adjust its reward system to honor the passions and accomplishments of its members.

CASE 6: What Is the Meaning of Passion in Your Life and Work?

You have recently returned from a convention on the importance of passion in your life in general and in the organization in particular. As a result of this staff development experience, you have had an internal dialogue, indeed debate, concerning the upside and downside of passion.

You have noted that leaders who exhibit their passion in a straightforward and dramatic way can motivate people in the organization, and yet their very passion has sometimes led to excesses. At the seminar, plenty of examples were gives of such excesses from CEOs to presidents of the United States.

The major question in your mind is simply, "What is the meaning of passion in my own life and work?"

_____

_____

_____

_____

_____

_____

Authors' Recommendations

The charismatic leader who demonstrates passion in a dramatic way is often the kind of leader who is featured in settings such as conventions. You are wise to remind yourself that these charismatic leaders are interesting in large measure because their lives are so full of contradictions. For example, they may exhibit love and understanding in one setting, such as a large group speech, but show mean-spiritedness in their personal lives. Or they may be admired for their dynamic speech on social concerns, and yet seem to be quite the opposite in one-on-one conversations. In short, they get media attention and interest precisely because of their inconsistencies.

We believe that a passion for one's work, a willingness to attend to the details of civility, and caring for others on a consistent basis are key elements of passion. And we also believe that curiosity is the driving force behind a leader's desire to learn, and it is precisely this commitment to learning and the welfare of others that will keep the effective leader's ego in proper perspective. It is this larger perspective that will serve you best in finding the meaning of passion in your life and work.

SELF INVENTORY

Now that you have completed the readings and activities on "The Power of Passion," think about what you've learned and respond to the following items on a five-point scale: 1 (low) to 5 (high).

---

1. My consciousness as to the power of passion for an activity or enterprise. _____

2. My ability to identify my strengths as a leader. _____

3. My ability to draw upon or use my strengths as a leader. _____

4. My willingness to leave my comfort zone in order to follow my passion for a personal goal. _____

5. My willingness to leave my comfort zone in order to follow my passion for an organizational goal. _____

6. My consciousness as to how personal "breakdowns" and suffering can lead to personal breakthroughs. _____

7. My consciousness as to how organizational "breakdowns" can lead to organizational breakthroughs. _____

8. My consciousness as to how passion has helped me and can help me to set aside or work through fears, anxieties, and self-doubt. _____

9. My consciousness that passion must be consistent, persistent,   _____
    and disciplined in order to avoid fickleness and faddism.

10. My consciousness that passion can intensify life by giving   _____
    attention to the seemingly small and mundane acts
    of simple kindnesses.

Note: If you are in a group setting, form discussion groups in order to share and summarize findings.

Scoring for Self Inventory

Total the ratings and find your score in the following scale:

41–50	Superior
31–40	Above Average
21–30	Average
11–20	Below Average
0–10	Poor

SUGGESTED READINGS

Graham, K. (1997). *Personal History.* New York: Vintage.

hooks, b. (1994). *Outlaw Culture: Resisting Representations.* New York: Routledge.

Morrison, A. M. (1992). *Breaking the Glass Ceiling: Can Women Reach the Top of America's Largest Corporations.* Reading, MA: Addison-Wesley.

Palmer, P. (2000). *Let Your Life Speak: Listening for the Voice of Vocation.* San Francisco: Jossey-Bass.

Schlesinger, A. M., Jr. (2000). *A Life in the Twentieth Century.* Boston: Houghton Mifflin.

Part II

The Leadership Journey

7

The Power of Hope

Dale L. Brubaker

Mrs. Birch, the director of food services in the university's student union, sat at her breakfast table surrounded by a few students, professors, and campus police. All were members of her "round table discussions." A motherly woman nearing retirement, Birch was known for helping students in need of money, food, and even housing. She was a person worth listening to, and those at her table drank their coffee and leaned forward in anticipation of her opening story:

> All of you know that I've been a member of a small rural church. Have been for years. We have a new, young minister fresh out of seminary at Duke. He is something! He has long hair, he dresses informally, and you won't believe it but he now has a processional and recessional, even though our church choir only has eight people in it. He doesn't stand behind the pulpit, but instead walks right out into the audience to give his sermon.
>
> And you should see his wife! She dresses like a hippie. She has this long, stringy hair and says pretty much what she thinks and doesn't care who hears it. She could care less about serving at teas in the parsonage, and she has all of these New Age posters that she painted displayed on the church walls.
>
> I'll tell you, they are something! You know why I like them? They are optimistic and that's exactly what this aging congregation needs!

Those of us sitting at her kitchen table were surprised at the punch line. It was obvious from her final comment that what we took for major issues were minor in Birch's mind, because the minister and his wife would bring life and a hopeful tone to a church that needed it.

In thinking about this conversation, it became clear to me that any group or person wants to think they can make a difference. Why would a person or organization want to follow a leader who has a vision of "gloom and doom"? A healthy person or organization certainly wouldn't support such a leader. The fact that a leader is hopeful doesn't mean that success is guaranteed, but the leader who isn't hopeful is a drag on the organization and oneself.

Eleanor Roosevelt is one of the first persons who comes to mind when I think about the power of hope. Her admonition to light a candle, rather than curse the darkness, graphically illustrates the story of her life. She realized through many difficult experiences that she had to change her own life in order to give leadership to changes that needed to be made in the world. Her own growth was phenomenal as she spoke out against social and political injustices. The unease in social situations that she had experienced throughout her life lessened as she courageously moved forward in the interest of those who were less fortunate. She had a political agenda and she was willing to use any contacts she had, including her husband, to further it. Explore writings about her in any bookstore or library, and you will be hard pressed to challenge the view that she is one of the most important women in American political history. Robin Gerber's book *Leadership the Eleanor Roosevelt Way* is a seminal work and one of this chapter's suggested readings, as is Roosevelt's 1961 autobiography.

It was in listening to a speech by Dr. Martin Luther King Jr. in Detroit on March 15, 1968—less than a month before his death on April 4, 1968—that I became aware of a distinction between hope and optimism. King was wary of some optimists who believed that things would naturally work out just fine without investing any resources in the process. He referred to this kind of optimism as "magic hope," a verbal slight of hand referring to leaders who denied the hard work necessary in order to accomplish an important goal such as civil rights. These optimists ventured into the land of "Pollyanna," the popular heroine of a 1913 novel for children who played "the glad game."

I encountered such optimism upon the death of my mother. "I'm really sorry abut your mother's death. How old was she?" commented an acquaintance. "Eighty," I replied. "Oh, then, she lived a good life," the acquaintance said. The conversation abruptly ended. Upon the stillbirth of our first grandchild, a similar encounter took place. "I know your son and daughter-in-law will have more children" was the only comment made by the acquaintance.

These comments weren't mean spirited, and they probably weren't meant to be uncaring. What is an alternative to superficial optimism, an alternative that is essential to our spiritual growth? King believed that hope is indispensable but that it must be accompanied by a realistic assessment of the situation, hard work, and the giving of whatever resources are at our disposal in order to meet our goals and our vision for ourselves and the organization.

The gift to oneself and others that comes from this commitment is love that is not afraid to feel the pain experienced by others and ourselves. Instead of sidestepping pain, we let ourselves feel it head on, and in making ourselves vulnerable we share more of our feelings and ideas with each other. In short, we connect rather than run away.

The realistic but hopeful leader knows this understanding and behavior can't be forced on others, but they can be a living example that others may or may not choose to follow. It is counterproductive to "sermonize" profusely or try to back insensitive others into a corner, but by "walking the talk," each of us can make a difference in our own lives and perhaps the lives of others.

Finally, what does all of this mean for leadership effectiveness and development? Turn to almost any research on this subject and you will find that interpersonal relationships are at the center of our success or lack of success as leaders. The leader who is realistic and hopeful will make a positive difference in the organization's present and future. Hopefulness can indeed be an important source of power.

Implications for Leaders

Larry D. Coble

ORIENTATION

Several years ago, a close family member was in the hospital with terminal cancer. While visiting at the hospital, I ran into my personal physician and told him of the pending circumstances and that the patient's oncologist had commented to me about his frustration. The oncologist had shared that, in his sixteen years of treating cancer patients, this cancer was one of the most aggressive that he had ever seen. My personal physician, a very wise man, took me aside and told me never to allow my loved one to give up hope.

In reflection, I can characterize my personal physician's action as a lesson in leadership. This example of trying to give hope to a terminally ill patient destined to die within days is quite dramatic and, perhaps, not couched in a realistic assessment of the situation. However, it does offer a glimpse of how important the power of hope can be. An anonymous writer once said, "Hope is the anchor of the soul, the stimulus to action, and the incentive to achievement."

A leader must offer realistic appraisal of each situation. Some would call this leadership action the defining of reality. It is, however, also a leadership responsibility to offer hope to individuals within the organization and hope for a better organization. Napoleon Bonaparte captured this idea when he referred to a leader as a "dealer in hope."

LEADERSHIP AS GIFT GIVING

Lee Bolman and Terrence Deal, in their wonderfully acclaimed book, *Leading With Soul*, make reference to the fact that leadership is gift giving, and that one of the gifts leaders can give is the gift of love. In order to give the gift of love, a leader must be a caring and compassionate leader. I believe that for a leader to effectively recognize and use the power of hope, the leader must understand this concept and know how closely hope and love are related.

Empathizing: Thinking Versus Feeling

A major implication for leaders in practicing the power of hope is to develop the ability to go beyond sympathizing with the people in your organization to an arena where you can actually empathize with your co-workers, subordinates, and even your boss. Due to our individual personality make-up, the ability to empathize comes more naturally for some of us than others. In fact, in having led hundreds of leadership development seminars for thousands of leaders, I can state without reservation that, on personality inventories, approximately 75 percent of leaders in our seminars have a preference for thinking over feeling. This, of course, doesn't mean that these leaders don't have feelings; it means that in the course of leading, they prefer to use thinking in problem solving as opposed to feeling. The real issue here is that so many of their subordinates are "feeling types" and that, when leaders use their heads instead of their hearts, they think they know how their subordinates feel.

My personality type indicates that I have a slight preference for thinking over feeling in problem solving. I can tell you for sure that, unless you are aware of your preferences and can figure out a way to balance them, your leadership will be dramatically less effective than it could be. Let me be more specific. Preferences for thinking or feeling in problem solving exist in degrees. Some people have a strong preference for one approach over the other. For example, a leader with a strong preference for thinking over feeling will want to deal with only the facts, logic, and what's rational. A leader with a strong preference for feeling will be most concerned with how she and others feel about the situation and what values are coming into play.

It has been my experience that organizations have rewarded leaders with promotions who tend to value thinking over feeling. The problem with this is that, as we go about "leading," we frequently underestimate how our followers feel about what we're doing. As I stated earlier, my personal preference is only slightly stronger for thinking than feeling, and yet the challenges that I faced in formal leadership roles could have been potentially disastrous if I had not recognized that most of the people on whom my decisions fell were people who were more feeling than thinking. You can imagine the magnitude of this issue when the leader's preferences are extremely high for thinking over feeling.

You will enhance your effectiveness and, ultimately, overall leadership if you recognize that you must be able to forecast how others will *feel* about your actions. Giving the people in your organization "more data" will not make them more responsive to your leadership, and, in general, it is not the path to using the power of hope. Keep a trusted colleague close to you who prefers feeling to thinking and who will tell you the truth. Have him or her help you forecast how people will feel about your latest bright idea, and then make adjustments accordingly.

FOLLOWERSHIP

The needs of the people under your leadership are varied and many. Those who tend to be the most satisfied are those whose individual needs can be met in a way that addresses the needs of the organization at the same time. Hopes have a better chance of being realized when they are compatible with the vision, mission, and objectives of the organization. Hope without action equates to unproductive idle dreams; hope becomes reality through realistic planning and implementing.

Your direct reports and peers will want to work in a nurturing environment that is grounded in trust. Your subordinates will want to know that the boss, and that's *you*, truly cares about them as human beings and not just what they can produce for the organization. A leader who deals in hope is a leader who cultivates a caring environment that focuses on people first over task completion. You must strive to establish a relationship with your followers that takes into account their psychological needs for support if you are going to be able to offer them hope. You also need to be aware that your hopes and the hopes of your followers will be ineffective unless they are shared and emphasized. You must lead your organization through the establishment of a culture that promotes and supports this kind of exchange.

THE CHANGE PROCESS

All leaders face obstacles in leading organizational change. Some of your followers will feel that they are no longer competent to do what the organization needs to have done. Some of your followers will be confused about how their specific role fits into the proposed change. Some will prefer to challenge your authority and may do so publicly or go underground with a covert sabotaging of the change efforts. Some of your followers will feel that the change means that they are going to have to give up something that was very important to them and, in turn, will suffer significant loss. Regardless of the leadership challenges that you face in leading change, it is your responsibility to offer hope for a better future for those involved in the process.

Change is a natural by-product of hope, and hope implies change. Hope cannot be realized without change, and change cannot be realized without some element of risk. Obstacles and hardships are overcome because leaders have an unwavering belief that conditions can and will improve. In leading the change process, it is helpful to interpret hopes in terms of realistic measurable objectives. This helps move from vague dreams to realistic goals.

CONCLUSION

The power of hope captures our belief that, whatever our challenge, we stand a chance of making success attainable. Strive to involve others in endorsing and implementing strategies to realize dreams. Move thought to action through acceptance and team effort. Study how other effective leaders have used the power of hope to overcome critical leadership challenges. Remember that hope is the ingredient that makes visions become reality.

ENGAGING SELF AND OTHERS

The following activities and materials are designed to involve you, the reader, and others, as you and they create learning communities. Because our major emphasis in this book is on leadership lessons for adults, the exercises focus on adult learning.

Activity 7.1

Take time to explore the concept that hope without action is a useless preoccupation. If you accept this concept, discuss the steps that are necessary to make those things that are hoped for become a reality. What does goal setting have to do with realizing hopes and dreams?

Activity 7.2
How Do You Cope When Things That
Are Hoped for Are Not Realized?

Answer the following questions:

Do you stop hoping and dreaming? If so, when and why?

Do you alter and change your dreams and hopes?

Do you change your strategies for realizing your hopes and dreams?

Do you make excuses or blame others because your hopes were not realized?

Activity 7.3

An organization without hope is an organization without a future. Our attention in this section of the book is to focus on those factors that produce and sustain hope in the person and the organization.

Identify those forces in your personal life that produce and sustain hope.

_____

_____

_____

_____

Leadership Seminar Participant Responses:

Those who love me, family and friends in particular.

My religion and spiritual life.

New ideas in a variety of fields of interest.

Exercise.

New challenges that stretch me but can be met.

Hobbies that give me a change from my work.

Identify those forces in your organizational life that produce and sustain hope.

_____

_____

_____

Leadership Seminar Participant Responses:

Leaders who are competent and care about me as well as the organization.

New challenges that are meaningful and doable.

Colleagues who know what they are doing and are good team members.

Opportunities to have learning experiences outside of the organization—for example, attend conferences and gain new ideas.

Networking online with some bright people outside of my organization.

Rewards—financial and other than financial. Promotions.

Activity 7.4a

Interpersonal relationships, when they are healthy, can be an important source of hope and happiness in an organization. When interpersonal relationships go wrong, they can work against an organization's goals and mission.

List interpersonal problems with *leaders* that you have experienced or observed.

_____

_____

_____

_____

Leadership Seminar Participant Responses:

Distance between what they say and what they do. Rhetoric and action aren't consistent.

Micromanagement. Some delegate and then look over your shoulder all the time and tell you what to do. Lack of trust is communicated.

No clear agenda leaves us with the feeling that he doesn't know what to do.

Strong on theory but lacking in practical knowledge.

Poor communication skills.

Changes direction in mid-stream—too many abrupt changes.

It is interesting how respondents immediately focused on inappropriate behavior on the part of the leader with their comments. In other words, respondents expected the leader to use his or her positional authority to set the tone for effective interpersonal relationships.

Activity 7.4b

List interpersonal relationship problems with *colleagues* that you have experienced or observed.

_____

_____

_____

_____

Leadership Seminar Participant Responses:

Incompetent—simply can't be counted on to do the work well.

Too pushy. Assumes authority not given. A control freak. Too outspoken.

Leaves us with the impression that he has a special relationship with those in higher positions that gives him special advantage.

Indiscreet. Things told in confidence are not held in confidence.

Seems to thrive on others' problems.

Always has to be the center of attention. Talks too much about himself and doesn't listen or seem to care about others.

A whiner. Always seems to see himself as victim.

It is interesting that those who made these responses locate the problem in the colleague and don't see interpersonal relationship problems as part of a two-way dynamic with a life of its own.

CASE 7: Creative Leadership, the Primacy of Interpersonal Relationships, and the Power of Hope

You and a few of your colleagues have been invited to a roundtable discussion at a nearby university on the subject of leadership effectiveness. You find the dialogue between those of you who are "on the firing line" and the academics quite interesting.

One professor presents the following view, which you find especially thought provoking: "Leadership is often defined as getting others to do what you want them to do whether or not they wish to do it. Creative leadership, however, is using your talents to help others discover and use their talents." The speaker concludes her thoughts with a quote from page 22 in *The Lessons of Experience*, by Morgan McCall, Michael Lombardo, and Ann Morrison: "In college I used my intellectual skills to get good grades by knowing the right answers. But at work, I found out that knowing the right answer was only 10 percent of the battle. Working with people was the other 90 percent. And we hadn't learned that at school."

You are intrigued as to the relationship between the professor's definition of creative leadership and the quote in *The Lessons of Experience*. What connections do you see and how might they be valuable for you as a creative leader?

_____

_____

_____

_____

_____

_____

Authors' Recommendations

The professor's view that many leaders have used their positional authority to give top-down orders that they expect to be followed in an efficient way certainly describes the traditional leadership paradigm. In recent years, however, a good deal of attention has been given to teamwork and shared decision making. It is interesting to note how an emphasis on helping others identify and use their talents fits with this newer view of leadership.

The McCall, Lombardo, and Morrison quote describes the traditional classroom setting in higher education. Taking notes from the professor's lectures and knowing the right answer on so-called objective tests was the order of the day. It is obviously more time consuming and resource demanding to provoke thought that is not easily tested. We believe this discussion between practitioners "on the firing line" and academics needs to be extended.

The primacy of interpersonal relations leads us to the hard work required in order to creatively lead during difficult times in our organizations. This hard work, however, gives us hope for a better future.

SELF INVENTORY

Now that you have completed the readings and activities on "The Power of Hope," think about what you've learned and respond to the following items on a five-point scale: 1 (low) to 5 (high).

1. My belief that hope is a necessary precondition for personal growth and effectiveness. _____

2. My belief that hope is a necessary precondition for organizational growth and effectiveness. _____

3. My belief that some optimists aren't willing to do the hard work necessary in order to address real problems. _____

4. My willingness to confront and feel the pain that life often brings to my personal life outside of the organization in which I work. _____

5. My willingness to confront and feel the pain that the organization I work for experiences. _____

6. My willingness to assess the distance between my personally stated goals and my actions. _____

7. My willingness to assess the distance between my organization's stated goals and its actions. _____

8. My recognition that making myself vulnerable often leads to a sharing with others that can be productive. _____

9. My understanding that what I do often makes more of a difference than what I say. _____

10. My belief that interpersonal relationships are central to leadership effectiveness and development. _____

Note: If you are in a group setting, form discussion groups in order to share and summarize findings.

Scoring for Self Inventory
Total the ratings and find your score in the following scale:

41–50	Superior
31–40	Above Average
21–30	Average
11–20	Below Average
0–10	Poor

SUGGESTED READINGS

Gerber, R. (2003). *Leadership the Eleanor Roosevelt Way*. New York: Portfolio.

Greene, M. (1998). *A Light in Dark Times*. New York: Teachers College Press.

Grogan, M. (1996). *Voices of Women Aspiring to the Superintendency*. Albany: State University of New York Press.

King, M. L., Jr. (2000). *The Autobiography of Martin Luther King, Jr.* (C. Carson, Ed.). New York: Warner Books.

McCall, M. W., Jr., Lombardo, M., & Morrison, A. (1988). *The Lessons of Experience*. Lexington, MA: Lexington Books.

Roosevelt, E. (1992). *Autobiography of Eleanor Roosevelt*. New York: Da Capo Press. (Original work published 1961)

8

The Power of
Keeping the Fire

Dale L. Brubaker

M ike is a veteran high school principal in his fifties—a time in his career when he has neither the enthusiasm of the beginner nor the clear vision of a person nearing retirement. It's Monday morning and he has hit the snooze button on his clock radio three times before swinging one leg out of bed, hoping the other will follow. He goes into the kitchen hoping that a glass of orange juice will wake him up, only to spill it on the floor. After running the dish rag across the floor, the juice is still sticky underfoot. Mike knows this is going to be another one of those days.

After performing his morning ritual, Mike gets in his car and drives toward the high school in order to arrive two hours before the students. As he approaches the circular drive in front of the school, an amazing thing happens. His car simply moves around the circle and heads toward home. He says to himself, "I won't do anybody any good today. I'm going home. I'll call in sick." He parks his car in the garage, walks into the house, and crawls back into bed.

Half an hour later, Mike gets dressed and returns to school, this time parking his car in its usual space, and enters the building. Sitting behind his desk, Mike starts softly singing John Lennon's 1980 hit "Watching the Wheels." After singing "I tell them there's no hurry, I'm just sitting here doing time," Mike stops, smiles, and wonders what it would take to get back and keep the fire he once had.

We've all been in Mike's shoes at one time or another. Work, whether at home or outside the home, becomes the same ol' same ol'—resulting in boredom. William F. Buckley reminds us in his 1976 book, *Airborne*, that "boredom is the deadliest poison, and it is a truism that it strikes hardest at the most comfortable."[1] And hard on the heels of boredom often comes cynicism, a deadly and cowardly form of superiority.

FINDING THE FIRE

The first step in finding and keeping the fire is the one that Mike took: recognize and accept where you are and the feelings associated with it. This is the starting place in dealing with the challenge ahead of you.

One of the things we learn with age and experience is that moving toward the pain is a necessary part of solving a problem. A prominent leader nearing retirement shared this wisdom: "So much of my early career was spent in denying and avoiding problems. Now I see that this was a waste of my resources. It was in addressing problems that I learned the most, and in the process of solving problems, I gained confidence in my leadership ability."

A second step in the process is asking yourself, "What are my special talents?"

Using your talents is a matter of interest and proficiency. In leadership seminars, participants are often asked to list their interests in one column and their proficiencies in another. The possible distinction between the two was brought to my attention during a meeting with Gerald Austin, a National Football League referee and education consultant. As I left his office, I said to him, "How about you making the phone call to this CEO? I'm not good at this sort of thing." Gerald responded, "No, you're good at it; you just don't especially enjoy doing it." He was right. I had little interest in or desire to make this call.

A good deal of pressure can be associated with being expected to do well at something you're good at. A talented tennis player shared why he enjoyed swimming: "I'm not expected to be good at it. It's simply a matter of swimming laps at my own speed, using an adequate but not outstanding swimming stroke."

A third step in finding and keeping the fire is deciding your degree of commitment to the changes that will need to be made in order to use your talents in particular settings. Roland Nelson, formerly at the Center for Creative Leadership, constructed a Commitment Scale. Consider which level of commitment you are willing to meet in order to move forward:

1. I will sacrifice my life and/or the lives of my family and/or those I dearly love.

2. I will give up the respect of those whom I love and I'll forego my status and professional achievement.

3. I will forego economic security and my career.

4. I will have serious conflicts between what I think should be done and my willingness to do it. I may have to alter my work style and give up those techniques that have previously been successful and beneficial in order to learn new ones.

5. I will have to alter some habits with which I'm quite comfortable, thus making my job somewhat more difficult. I will feel uncomfortable from time to time, as I'll do things that don't seem to be the best way to do them based on my past experience and present assumptions.

6. It doesn't make any difference what past experiences may indicate. My choice, therefore, is between Tweedledee and Tweedledum.

Mike, the high school principal, decided to leave his position and begin work on a doctorate in an area outside of education. In order to do this, he made a level 3 commitment: he was willing to forego economic security and his career. (Most leaders we've known have made level 4 or 5 commitments in order to use their talents in different ways.)

It's important to remember that large, dramatic steps are not always necessary in order to gain the confidence needed for larger leadership roles. One participant who attended a leadership seminar described a step that he had taken that seemed particularly significant:

The chair of a committee asked who wanted to take the minutes [at a meeting]. Heads turned downward and no one volunteered. I said that I would, and I soon discovered that I could write interesting and sometimes humorous notes. This record was always read at the beginning of each meeting. Thus, I played a part in setting the tone for the committee's work. I was part of the action.

The interesting thing about practicing leadership skills is that it leads to self-assurance and enjoyment. And there's a bonus—best expressed by professional golfer Gary Player: "The harder I practice, the luckier I get."[2]

The personal and professional rewards in meeting the challenges described in this chapter are many, but perhaps the most satisfying one is to participate in something larger than oneself. For it is in using the talents that interest us that we create each other in community.

Implications for Leaders

Larry D. Coble

ORIENTATION

Many leaders become fixated at a particular stage in their own development. For these leaders, the "pay-off" for leading is virtually the same in every job. They like the trappings of the executive suite; as they move through the leadership chairs, they are after bigger and better perks. It seems that we have an epidemic of failing corporations, but we continue to see CEOs walk away with untold millions in their bank accounts when, at the same time, their employees' pension plans have dried up and stock prices have fallen off the charts. Also, we sometimes see similar behavior in leaders who reside in the not-for-profit or education sector. Even though leaders in these types of organizations don't have stock options, there is a pecking order that delineates which organizations are likely to offer the best "package." Frequently, then, it is the "package" that becomes the incentive for moving to another job.

If you find yourself sharing some of the above-mentioned aspirations, it's okay. Just recognize that unless your needs are changing, then you are not growing and developing as a human being and as a leader. For me, the salary and perks were never enough. They had to be paired with the ever-increasing challenges that go with leading larger and more complex organizations. I actually once told the members of the Chamber of Commerce in a large southern city that I was changing jobs because I wanted "to run as much of the world as I possibly could." Taking on the challenges and the perks that went with it was who I was at the time. As my needs changed, I elected to leave that type of leadership position. What is of extreme importance, however, is to note that whether I was leading a large organization, a small consulting firm, or myself, it was my responsibility to keep the fire ignited in myself and in those working under my leadership. A fundamental aspect of leadership is to recognize and effectively use the power of keeping the fire.

THE EXPANSIVE PERSONALITY

Of the truly "driven" leaders with whom I have been well acquainted, including myself, every one tends toward expansive personality types. In other words, we are individuals who like doing things on a grand scale. The bigger the challenge, the better we like it. We love going where angels fear to tread. Psychologists would say that leaders of this nature have their sense of self-worth tied up in their ability to achieve at very high levels. What tends to keep the fire ignited in leaders of this type is a "higher and faster" roller coaster ride. Those of us who fit this description need to recognize that life at the office will work if we continue to take on more and more responsibility. For us, the pay-off is mastering challenge after challenge, especially those that appear to others to require almost super-human feats. Our work is central to our life. Nothing is quite as important to us as is our work.

With our work so central to our identity and with the pay-offs that we get from our careers, it should be of little surprise, then, that we have difficulty achieving high levels of intimacy in our relationships, especially with spouses, children, and significant others. For so many of us, it is once again the presence of those early childhood experiences that have shaped and influenced us. Our drive, perhaps, comes from a deep-seated insecurity that stems from some type of troubled childhood that manifests itself in our adult lives as a need to attain hero status. The good news, however, is that the match between driven leaders and executive leadership positions is just about perfect. Individuals need the challenges and the perks that go with such positions; the positions need the talent, determination, drive, and skill set of the leader.

In order to keep the fire alive in yourself and in those you lead who share a similar set of needs, you need to continue taking on that next challenge and the next one after that. You will need a reward system that is commensurate with what you believe to be fair, based on your contributions. You will eventually get to the point that the amount of money and the perks are less important than if you perceive that those who control the rewards are truly recognizing and appreciating your talents and your contributions. This will also be true for those you lead. Take heart. There are others out there like you.

Based on a lot of experience and much pain and personal frustration, I warn you: do not try to run your home like you run your office. You have been successful, so, in all likelihood, your children will not have experienced the hardships that you have experienced and therefore will not be as driven as you have been. Don't impose your standards on them and on your spouse. You don't realize it yet, but your standards are tough, and it is nearly impossible for people to measure up. Many will try to measure up, and perhaps will try for a very long time, but, all the while, resentments are building and eventually the cost to you and your personal life will be very high. Some leaders are so egocentric that they don't care. Don't be one of those people. Remember that most of the world is more interested in high-quality relationships than the bottom line, and that includes the people in your personal life.

MAKING AN INNER SHIFT AND KEEPING THE FIRE ALIVE

My guess is that you know someone, or have at least heard of someone, who voluntarily gave up a powerful and high-profile leadership position and all the trappings of the office. What frequently occurs is that these individuals go through some type of soul-searching experience and make an inner shift that allows them to begin to think of ways that they can enjoy life in a different way and not have to depend so much on their achievements. They become more satisfied with what they have accomplished. They are more satisfied with their material possessions, and they become more interested in establishing closer, more intimate relationships with the most important people in their lives. This may happen to you. It did happen to me. And even though this happens, you must continue to keep the fire alive.

When I decided to step down from a high-profile leadership position, my friends and colleagues said that it would never last. They said that I needed the television cameras and the newspaper reporters following me around to feed my ego. What they didn't realize was that, over time, my needs had changed and that I had spent considerable time and effort in thinking about how to keep the fire. My conclusion was that, in order for me to keep the fire, I needed a different kind of challenge. That challenge turned out to be designing and delivering leadership training and development programs for a world-class organization and teaching at a university. I continued to achieve, but with less mental, physical, and emotional wear and tear. You must be true to yourself. If you need the roller coaster ride, then get on and stay on and realize the pay-offs, the perks, and the liabilities that go with it. If you need a different kind of ride, then be honest enough with yourself to make a change, but be responsible for figuring out ways that will keep the fire alive in you.

In order to keep the fire alive, you must become increasingly self-aware. You must constantly question your motives for your actions. Strive to understand the reasons behind your behavior. Seek feedback from trusted colleagues and listen and internalize their responses. Ask for honest feedback and take it in the spirit that is intended, to help you grow.

I believe that understanding the reasons behind your behavior is more important than the behavior itself. By becoming more self-aware and more reflective, you enhance the possibility of becoming more adaptable and developing a better understanding of your limitations. You may also recognize, as I did, that you may have the experience and skill set for that next "faster ride," but you just are no longer willing to pay the price because your needs have changed. As you become more self-aware, you will recognize what has to be present in order for you to keep the fire alive.

CONCLUSION

A strong possibility exists that, at some point in your career, you will lose the fire for your job if you do not seek new challenges and get out of your comfort zone. One of the best ways to continue to enjoy your job enthusiastically is to become involved in productive change activities. One of your major responsibilities as a leader is to plan and implement strategies designed to keep yourself motivated and to create conditions for your subordinates to become more motivated. If you appear to be bored with your life and your job, there is a chance that your followers will emulate your behavior. It should be noted that systems leadership theory suggests that we strongly underestimate our importance as role models for our followers and overestimate the importance of our intelligence.

Lead the transition to an organizational culture that is characterized by enthusiasm for work and a zest for life in general. Create goals that will continue to challenge your followers to perform at peak levels. Act as the chief cheerleader for your organization, employing the style that feels right for you.

ENGAGING SELF AND OTHERS

The following activities and materials are designed to involve you, the reader, and others, as you and they create learning communities. Because our major emphasis in this book is on leadership lessons for adults, the exercises focus on adult learning.

Activity 8.1

For the last three years, your organization has failed to attain several important goals. As a result, the morale of your personnel has suffered. As the leader of the organization, what steps will you take to keep the fire "burning" among your employees?

_____

_____

_____

_____

_____

_____

_____

Activity 8.2

An appraisal review team has recently issued an evaluation report of your organization to the Board of Directors. Among the findings was a statement that many of your employees were suffering from burnout. You do not agree with this finding. What can you do to determine whether the finding is valid? If valid, how do you go about determining the cause of the burnout?

_____

_____

_____

_____

_____

_____

Activity 8.3

Indicate with a check mark whether you employ each of the following behaviors/principles in leading your organization.

- ❑ I make every effort to create challenges that will take me out of my comfort zone.
- ❑ I respect and promote workers who demonstrate enthusiasm for their jobs.
- ❑ When appropriate, I will implement positive change to eliminate boredom on the job.
- ❑ I attempt to create an organizational culture that builds enthusiasm among workers.
- ❑ I use inspirational speakers and other techniques to "keep the fire alive" in my organization.
- ❑ I act as a cheerleader to create and maintain enthusiasm in my organization.
- ❑ I include enthusiasm as one of the positive indicators of performance of workers on the job.
- ❑ I use stretching goals to encourage workers to enthusiastically seek to improve throughout their careers.

Activity 8.4
Expansive Leader Inventory

Instructions

To assist you in identifying the type of expansive leader you might be, assign ratings to the 36 statements below by indicating the extent to which they describe you.

3 = To a Great Extent

2 = To Some Extent

1 = To a Little or No Extent

After completing the inventory, follow the instructions for scoring and interpreting your responses.

Statement	Rating
1. I tend to devote considerable time and energy making sure that I make a positive impression on people.	3 2 1
2. At times my motivation is to dispel a personal sense of inadequacy.	3 2 1

Statement	Rating
3. I need to be right, to be above reproach.	3 2 1
4. I place a great deal of emphasis on public relations.	3 2 1
5. I am motivated to correct or fix things that are not working well.	3 2 1
6. Adhering to my principles is very important.	3 2 1
7. I enjoy being esteemed or admired by others.	3 2 1
8. My parents actively diminished or mistreated me.	3 2 1
9. I continually try to do right and expect others to do the same.	3 2 1
10. I strive to build organizations worthy of high praise and admiration.	3 2 1
11. I sometimes have a sense of being unworthy.	3 2 1
12. I am often on the lookout for nonadherence in the way things are supposed to be done by myself and others.	3 2 1
13. My parents had very high expectations for me.	3 2 1
14. I am often a tough, unrelenting taskmaster.	3 2 1
15. I am vigilant.	3 2 1
16. I believe that my Board of Directors has very high expectations for me.	3 2 1
17. I am reluctant to offer support and praise to my subordinates.	3 2 1
18. I am attentive to detail, sometimes tending toward obsession.	3 2 1
19. My parents lavished attention and praise on me.	3 2 1
20. I tend toward being intolerant of anything but the highest performance.	3 2 1

Statement	Rating
21. I have a very strong conscience.	3 2 1
22. I strive to be number one in all spheres of my life.	3 2 1
23. I tend to often focus on what is wrong even when things are going well.	3 2 1
24. I identify fervently with the ideal world and am troubled by the existence of imperfection.	3 2 1
25. I often enjoy flaunting my successes.	3 2 1
26. I never stop pushing for fear of losing motivation.	3 2 1
27. My parents were exacting, principled people.	3 2 1
28. I am highly competitive.	3 2 1
29. I weed out things that are substandard.	3 2 1
30. I tend toward being quick to criticize and reprimand others.	3 2 1
31. I put so much energy and time into relationships with key influentials that I have little time for relationships with peers and subordinates.	3 2 1
32. I tend to strive towards dominance.	3 2 1
33. I tend to be opinionated and sometimes self-righteous.	3 2 1
34. I tend to view myself in a favorable light despite occasional feedback to the contrary.	3 2 1
35. I view most things as being in need of fixing.	3 2 1
36. I tend to be obsessive about minor things that are a matter of principle.	3 2 1

SCORING PROCEDURES

Record your ratings from the completed inventory and add up the three columns.

Striver-Builder	Self-Vindicator/ Fix-It Specialist	Perfectionist— Systematizer
Total =	Total =	Total =

INTERPRETATION OF SCORES

Scores for the three types can be interpreted in two ways. First, they can be interpreted solely on the basis of size or magnitude of the ratings as follows:

High:	Score at or above 25
Average:	Score between 16 and 24
Low:	Score at or below 15

Second, a rating for a particular style can be interpreted relative to the size of the ratings of the other two expansive styles. For example, if a rating for a particular style is twice the size, or more, of the other two ratings combined, it can be considered a high rating. If the ratings for the three styles are similar in magnitude, it can mean that the leader does not have a predominant expansive leadership style.

COMPLEMENTARY COMMENTARY

Briefly, definitions of the three types of expansive leaders are:

- The *Striver-Builder* is the type of expansive leader who strives to impress other people. As managers, they specialize in building up organizations worthy of the high praise and admiration they want for themselves.

- The *Self-Vindicator/Fix-It Specialist* is the expansive leader who is motivated fundamentally by a need to dispel a sense of personal inadequacy. As adults, they may turn work and careers into campaigns to dispel themselves as being unworthy.
- The *Perfectionist-Systematizer* is the type of expansive leader who, above everything, needs to be right or above reproach. At their worst, these people can be opinionated and self-righteous.

RECOMMENDED DEVELOPMENTAL ACTION

The three expansive leaders may take the following actions to assure that they become more effective leaders:

Striver-Builder

- Strive to get beyond the heavy dependence on external recognition and come to personal acceptance of oneself.
- Learn to get satisfaction out of committing themselves fully to something or someone outside of themselves.
- Transcend the compelling need to look good at all costs.
- Overcome the tendency to take credit not due them or to withhold credit due to others.
- Invest heavily in self-improvement activities.

Self-Vindicator/Fix-It Specialist

- Gain a measure of self-acceptance that allows them to temper their tough, demanding nature with a measure of supportiveness.
- Develop a better appreciation of what is valuable about people.
- Reduce the compulsion to root out anything and everything substandard.
- Learn to channel their drive into selective improvement of things that are genuinely in need of improvements.

Perfectionist-Systematizer

- Learn to be guided by their principles but not be tyrannized by them.
- Lead on the basis of personal principles but accept principles that may be different.
- Work successfully with people who hold different principles from theirs.
- Harness a sense of order to constructive ends.
- Get beyond the attachment to form for its own sake and put it to work infusing their units with needed structure and definition.

Activity 8.5a

Finding and keeping the fire can be a challenging and rewarding issue in your personal and organizational life. Briefly describe where you are in your career with regard to this important issue.

_____

_____

_____

_____

_____

Activity 8.5b

As you consider where you have been on this matter in the past and as you share with others where you have been, are, and want to be in keeping the fire, it will be clear to you that life and one's career have different stages. A seminar participant shared the following with us: "When I began my career, I was so busy that keeping the fire wasn't an issue. When I arrived at the midpoint in my career, I realized that my occasional boredom resulted, in part, because I knew the shortcuts that gave me more time for introspection. I am at a point now where I can retire, and I find that I am so busy preparing for my own reinvention that I am once again busier than ever. Boredom is not an issue."

List the forces that contributed to your having "the dream" of success when you began your career.

_____

_____

_____

_____

_____

Leadership Seminar Participant Responses:

Teachers and university professors saw me as a person with talents who could go somewhere in my profession.

University courses in my major made me aware of positions to which I could aspire.

There was a good deal of competition among us in my major at the university— especially in graduate school where we were ranked in our class.

Although we were civil to each other, those of us who were hired fought for the rewards in the organization. The norms for getting to the top were fairly clearly made known to us when we began to work there.

We heard stories about those who had made it in my profession and those who didn't. I simply thought of myself as one who would make it. I dwelt on my strengths and successes and gave little attention to what could go wrong. I had been raised to believe that success breeds self-confidence, which, in turn, leads to more success.

My parents had a "can do" attitude toward themselves and their children.

I found "the dream" to be very motivating and vowed to continue to have it as long as I could.

COMPLEMENTARY COMMENTARY

These comments help us see the role of "the dream" in getting or finding and keeping the fire.

Activity 8.5c

With time and experience in our careers, we see in others and ourselves the forces that lead to a kind of erosion of "the dream." List the forces that you have identified.

_____

_____

_____

_____

_____

Leadership Seminar Participant Responses:

I discovered that there wasn't a good fit between my talents and what the organization rewarded. I had little real knowledge of the possibility of such a misfit when I joined this organization. I was so happy to get the job that I apparently ignored this reality.

I knew that I had the "right stuff" to make it at work. However, I discovered with time that I wouldn't have a life outside of work. A sixty-hour work week was too high a price to pay for making it.

I had little idea what it would be like to play politics in order to get to the top. My original dream was that I would do good work and be rewarded for it with promotion after promotion. Playing the game wasn't my cup of tea, and I chose to leave the organization.

I discovered that "the dream" was, in fact, my parents' dream. I wasn't cut out for this profession, and I'm glad that I discovered this in time to change course. My parents, of course, weren't happy about this, and conflict and some distance was the result until they began to understand where I was coming from.

Although being in this profession is financially rewarding and gives you a good deal of prestige, I can't think of anything that is much more boring than this job. It is ironic that people at cocktail parties fawn all over me simply because of my title. If they only knew how I retreat to my office in order to play the stock market just to avoid the boredom. I'm good at my job, but I would rather do something I am less good at, if it were interesting.

Activity 8.5d

We are now at the place where we can profit from concrete steps that need to be taken in order to avoid the erosion described in the previous comments. List the steps you have considered taking or have taken in order to do this.

_____

_____

_____

_____

_____

Leadership Seminar Participant Responses:

> I gave up my position in the organization and took a less prestigious one that was more in line with my talents and interests. It cost me some money, but I am happier now, and I will be able to stay the course. Although I am certified as a CPA, I am now a tour guide for people interested in our plant. I see myself as more of a teacher than anything else, and I really am enjoying meeting different people who tour the plant. I've discovered that it is enjoyable doing my homework in order to adjust my presentation to the particular group that is visiting the plant. I work for the same company, but I am in a different role.

> I couldn't take it any more! I quit, and after six months had another job more to my liking.

> Since I am just a few years away from retirement, I decided to continue in my present position doing an acceptable job that won't be an embarrassment to me or my company. I am throwing my energy and creativity into my hobby—small time farming. I have a few pictures in my dayplanner of my farm and various things I do there. During the day I can hardly wait to get on my tractor after work. I downplay my hobby at work, but people there seem to leave me alone, since I am doing an acceptable job, and they know I won't be there long. In fact, the other day, a younger colleague stopped by my office and measured it to see if his furniture will fit when I retire.

> I decided to bring life to my job by doing something about my weakest area of work—dissertation advising. A colleague, who is also a friend of mine, and I decided to take the steps necessary to prepare to write a book on the subject. After getting the knowledge I needed and organizing it, I was able to contribute to this two-year project. Because of reader interest in the first book, my colleague and I wrote a second book on the subject. Researching, writing, using these books with doctoral students—all brought new life to my career at precisely the time when I needed it.

COMPLEMENTARY COMMENTARY

You can see from these examples that different persons face the keeping the fire issue in different ways—some of which you will like and some of which you won't. However, the examples do serve us in seeing that the issue is very much alive for each of us at different times in our careers. As argued in the opening discussion of this chapter, seemingly small steps may be much more helpful to you than large, dramatic steps. It is important, when one doesn't have the fire, to do something rather than slipping into boredom and cynicism.

CASE 8: The Need for a "Jump Start," or Is It More Than This?

You are at the mid-point of your career. You are no longer driven by the dream you had when you took your first job, and you can't feel the reality of retirement—an event some time in the future. When you share your feelings of stagnancy with younger colleagues, they assure you of your success and basically tell you to snap out of it. Colleagues near retirement shake their heads and lament the number of years you still have to go. The freshness of your youth is gone, and yet you don't feel really old.

You know that you have been here before, but now it seems different. Throwing yourself into your work by becoming more task oriented and working longer hours no longer seems to work. You notice that your young colleagues throw themselves into the newly designated leader's strategic plan, and you recognize this fad or "flavor of the month" for what it is—a way for the new leader to make a name for himself.

You find yourself listening to the lyrics of popular songs by artists who are sharing their life stories. They, too, seem to feel sorry for themselves in describing their mid-life crises. You are conscious as to how friends in your neighborhood deal with their mid-life malaise. Most of them are caught up in buying more things—more expensive cars, moving up to the next, more affluent housing area and the like. Some turn to alcohol and other drugs as the answer to their problems.

These difficulties are compounded by the premature deaths of several of your friends and acquaintances. Heart attacks, cancer, and accidents have taken their toll, and you note at a recent class reunion that the number of fellow graduates is beginning to dwindle. The result of this is that you are beginning to think more seriously of your own mortality.

You are more than a little puzzled by all of this, and a question begins to emerge as you creatively brood about where you go from here: "Do I simply need a 'jump start,' or is it more than this?"

_____

_____

_____

_____

_____

Authors' Recommendations

Daniel Levinson and colleagues describe the reality of this situation in their classic books titled *The Seasons of a Man's Life* and *The Seasons of a Woman's Life*. Knowing that it is natural for you to feel as you do is certainly a helpful starting place. This realization is more than misery loving company. It is an understanding that can keep you from obsessing about your problems. Instead, you can see the possibilities of composing a more satisfying career and life.

You have used your talents to achieve the success you have experienced, and you now have the opportunity to work smarter and take on new challenges—many of which are small steps in new directions. It may be important for you to spend time with like-minded friends and colleagues who are facing or who have faced these challenges.

SELF INVENTORY

Now that you have completed the readings and activities on "The Power of Keeping the Fire," think about what you've learned and respond to the following items on a five-point scale: 1 (low) to 5 (high).

1. The extent to which I have acknowledged boredom as a personal problem that I need to address. _____

2. The extent to which I have acknowledged cynicism as a personal problem that I need to address. _____

3. The extent to which I value finding and keeping the fire in my personal life. _____

4. The extent to which I value finding and keeping the fire at work. _____

5. My awareness as to the possible distinction between my interests and my proficiencies (what I do well). _____

6. My awareness as to the possible distance between what I say my commitments are and what I am really willing to do. _____

7. My recognition that small steps or acts are often as important or more important than larger, more visible and dramatic acts. _____

8. My ability to identify what these small steps might be in my personal life. _____

9. My ability to identify what these steps might be in my organizational life. _____

10. My recognition that practicing leadership skills is an essential part of becoming an effective leader. _____

Note: If you are in a group setting, form discussion groups in order to share and summarize findings.

Scoring for Self Inventory

Total the ratings and find your score in the following scale:

41–50	Superior
31–40	Above Average
21–30	Average
11–20	Below Average
0–10	Poor

SUGGESTED READINGS

Brock, B. L. & Grady, M. L. (2000). *Rekindling the Flame: Principals Combating Teacher Burnout.* Thousand Oaks, CA: Corwin Press.

Curry, B. (2000). *Women in Power: Pathways to Leadership in Education.* New York: Teachers College Press.

Goleman, D. (1997). *Emotional Intelligence.* New York: Bantam Books.

Moxley, R. S. (2000). *Leadership and Spirit: Breathing New Energy Into Individuals and Organizations.* San Francisco: Jossey-Bass.

9

The Power of Determination

Dale L. Brubaker

L loyd DuVall, a prominent educational and governmental leader, learned as a child to combine musical talent and self-discipline. He began playing the piano in the second grade. With encouragement from his musical family, he soon performed "concertettes" for other classes in his school.

DuVall knew at the age of 8 that he wanted to play in the Ohio State University band. But, in his own words, "I was a terrible trumpet player." Fortunately, a new high school band director arrived a few years later and suggested that he switch to the tuba. In his junior year of high school, he won first place in state competition for playing a Bach violin sonata on the tuba. In his senior year, he auditioned for and gained entry to the Ohio State University School of Music.

DuVall's self-management skills integrated musicianship and athletic ability in the marching band at Ohio State University. He carried a 30-pound Sousaphone, swung his left arm, marched at 180 steps per minute, lifted each leg parallel to the ground on every step, and played music memorized for that week's performance. As a sophomore, he was named manager of the band.

As manager, he recognized the importance of personal satisfaction and group harmony. He learned that the leader creates the conditions for organizational effectiveness by communicating objectives and ways to reach them. DuVall was awarded the honor of being the dot in the *i* when the band spelled out *Ohio State* on the football field.

Upon graduation, DuVall became a band director. His leadership ability was quickly identified and he moved into administration. His success as an administrator led to a prestigious position at the University of Oregon where, with time, he burned out and needed time off. His request was denied, so he decided to move to Tennessee where he single-handedly built a log cabin. His volunteer work to improve this region of the country led to an Appalachian government position that challenged him to use his negotiating and networking skills.

Lloyd DuVall had a special interest in balancing individual effort with teamwork. As he told me in January 2000:

> I am intrigued by the role of personal pride in the organization and its influence on the quality of organizational performance. I remember the price band members paid at Ohio State for making serious mistakes during a Saturday performance. They were treated to an unceremonious dunking in the Olentangy River on Monday and would be forced to wear a sandwich board painted in the colors of archrival University of Michigan at every practice during the week. These standards were set and enforced by band members, not the director.

The success DuVall experienced in his life and career has been marked by an important source of power—*determination*, a firmness of purpose.

WHAT CREATES DETERMINATION WITHIN US?

DuVall's love of music, when coupled with talent and family encouragement, gave him an early start. He also realized that self-discipline—a commitment to hard work—was essential. Sentimentality would be no substitute for many long hours of practice. DuVall referred to such devotion as "self-management skills." In short, no person but oneself can do the kind of work essential to firmness of purpose.

At the same time, DuVall became intrigued with the importance of group harmony. He was not a "Lone Ranger." Rather, he realized that his example as a team leader set the tone for the entire community of band members. DuVall didn't flaunt his abilities. David Halberstam, author of *War in a Time of Peace*, cites Brent Scowcroft, former National Security Council chair and advisor to presidents, as an example of a person who didn't seek personal power or titles but instead brought intelligence, good judgment, and decency to his work. DuVall, like Scrowcroft, quietly went about his business in behalf of admirable purposes.

DuVall, although committed to his purposes, didn't believe that there was only one way to reach these goals. He was candid about his disappointment in not being a good trumpet player. This honesty made it possible for him to move on to an instrument, the tuba, in which he excelled. If he had felt victimized as a trumpet player, he would have been stuck in self-pity.

DuVall encountered another setback when he applied for, but didn't receive, a leave from an administrative job that led to his burnout. He could have simply accepted this defeat and stayed on the job to the considerable detriment of his physical and psychological health. His successful efforts to single-handedly build a log cabin gave him the change of scenery and setting to renew himself. As a result, he used his considerable networking skills to give leadership to people in rural Tennessee.

One of the most powerful examples of determination and the inner strength that creates it came to our nation's consciousness on December 1, 1955, when Rosa Parks refused to give up her seat to a white man on a segregated bus in Montgomery, Alabama. This event sparked the bus boycott in Montgomery. "The only tired I was, was tired of giving in," Rosa Parks said. Her determination didn't begin with this event, when she was 32 years old, however. She was an active worker in her local chapter of the National Association for the Advancement of Colored People (NAACP), working with youth groups and recording accounts of victims of hate crimes. As an assistant to Representative John Conyers in Detroit, she nearly lost her life in 1994 when she was beaten and robbed. Her life is brilliantly described by historian Douglas Brinkley in his book *Rosa Parks,* one of the suggested readings at the end of this chapter.

THE BENEFITS OF A LEADER'S DETERMINATION

The leader who communicates determination in behalf of worthwhile purposes gives members of an organization the good feeling and confidence that their efforts will be important and personally meaningful. Determination, therefore, has both a personal and organizational face.

Determination rooted in morality can benefit the person and the organization. In effect, the conscience of the person and organization is a compass that guides decision making.

Implications for Leaders

Larry D. Coble

ORIENTATION

Leaders who understand and use the power of determination have a magnificent obsession to do what's right for the organization and the people who work in it. Successful use of the power of determination over the long haul involves becoming obsessed about your work and staying obsessed. As I have reflected on my own determination, and the determination of successful leaders with whom I have worked closely, I recognize that a common factor among all those determined individuals was the presence of a *fear of failure*. These leaders did not want to fail at the job, regardless of the nature of the challenge. They never wanted to be perceived as not being able to do the job. I vividly recall telling my staff, regardless of the position that I held at the time, that I would do whatever necessary to do what was right and get the job done. I went on to say that I would "hug 'em, pat 'em on the back, or kick 'em in the butt," whatever it took. This was not intended to intimidate. It was just a fact. I meant what I said; I did what I felt I had to do. That is what leaders do. Leaders become engulfed by their leadership challenges, and their work becomes their play.

I want to mention here that just because leaders who are determined have a fear of failure doesn't mean that they have never failed or experienced hardships. We have already established that our development *requires* that we have hardships that enable us to grow. Determined leaders have had many hardships, many of which could be considered failures. They learn from them, but they don't like them. For determined leaders, disappointment is a feeling that they don't enjoy experiencing. What is also true is that these leaders are, by nature, risk-takers; because they will take on challenges that the average person would shy away from, they are more likely to experience failure. Their general attitude, however, is not to wish the challenge were easier; it is to wish that they were better prepared to tackle it.

WORK ETHIC

I once had an associate who said that some of our most vocal critics were people who, "if they can't find a god to love, they'll find a devil to hate." What he meant was that our vocal critics could actually get psyched up to oppose things that they didn't agree with or felt threatened by. Determined leaders may not find a devil to hate, but they certainly possess the power to "psyche themselves up." Leaders know where they are trying to go. They have an incredible ability to focus for long periods of time. They can stay in the moment but see the future. Leadership excellence demands loyalty to and responsibility for the challenge, but it gives back results. I can't overstate the importance of honestly facing up to the challenge, the work that must be done, the hard decisions that must be made, the people who must be terminated, and the people who must improve their performance to remain a part of the organization. Your leadership legacy cannot tolerate difficulty as an excuse.

THE LEADER'S NEED FOR CONTROL

As a formal leader, it is your responsibility to be the organization's primary caretaker and its chief change officer. What complicates all of this is the need to involve your stakeholders in preservation and change and your interpersonal need to be in control. A major implication for you is to develop a full and complete understanding of the nature of your need to be in control. In general, it has been my experience that leaders have a high need to be in charge. They like to take on responsibilities and enjoy directing subordinates under their supervision. What you need to watch out for here is whether your need to be in control is high, to the point that you are making decisions that others should be making, or if you want to be in control just for the sake of control.

Leaders with extreme needs to be in control of people and events tend to, more often than not, employ authoritarian approaches, frequently dwell on negativism, and fail to consider the importance of explaining reasons for, or understanding the consequence of, their actions. This type of extreme controlling behavior is disempowering for your subordinates.

Recognize that control is an interpersonal need that is psychologically based. Because it is an interpersonal need, it can change throughout your life. Using myself as an example, I can tell you that for most of my early and mid-career, I had a very high need to be in charge, to make decisions, to take on responsibility, and direct others. To be effective, you must have a strong need to be in charge. Also, to be effective, you must understand that it is imperative to get your control needs under control or people will resent you and will often sabotage your efforts. You may temporarily get compliance, but you will not get commitment. What you are after is commitment.

A very good combination of traits for a leader is to pair a relatively high need for control with very strong interpersonal skills. In fact, leaders with this combination are seldom viewed as being dictatorial or authoritarian, whereas those leaders who may be no more controlling but lack strong interpersonal skills are often viewed as tyrants. Make sure that you are able to take charge, know when to take charge, and enjoy being in charge, but share control through a more facilitative approach as circumstances warrant it. It is also important to mention that, if you get too involved in trying to control things over which you have little to no control, you will use so much energy that this will have an adverse affect on the things you should be trying to control.

CONCLUSION

To be successful in leadership, you must be talented; however, determination and drive are more important than talent. When a leader can combine talent and determination, he or she is unstoppable. You must bring to the leadership challenge a mindset of being uncompromising when it comes to doing what's right. You must be obsessed in your belief in what you are doing. If you are truly committed to leadership excellence, you will accept no excuses, only results. Set your expectations so much higher than those who pretend to want to lead, and then live up to your expectations.

ENGAGING SELF AND OTHERS

The following activities and materials are designed to involve you, the reader, and others, as you and they create learning communities. Because our major emphasis in this book is on leadership lessons for adults, the exercises focus on adult learning.

Activity 9.1

It is often stated that you can move mountains if you try hard enough and have determination. Is it possible that adherence to this belief could be detrimental to your followers? Is it possible that some goals are virtually unattainable and that it would take a miracle, despite the degree of determination, to realize success? What role does a leader have in setting realistic goals?

Activity 9.2

Reflect on past experiences to determine whether someone you know overcame severe hardships or reached "unattainable" goals because of pure determination and will power. What does this individual's accomplishments tell us about the power of determination?

Activity 9.3

Read each of the following practices and principles and place a check mark next to those you use in your role as a leader.

- ❑ Develop an organization culture that encourages determination and a strong will to succeed.
- ❑ Surround yourself with workers who have a strong determination to succeed.
- ❑ Reward personnel who exhibit strong determination.
- ❑ Take care not to assign tasks to individuals who are incapable of completing a job.
- ❑ Set examples of how determination can overcome serious obstacles.
- ❑ Judge performance on the basis of effort put forth as well as successful completion of tasks.
- ❑ Set goals that have realistic chances of being achieved.
- ❑ Refuse to accept failure as a deterrent to moving ahead.
- ❑ Provide motivational training that enhances staff's will to succeed.

Activity 9.4a

Determination is a firmness of purpose that can help you stay the course when you believe the purpose you are pursuing is worthwhile. You will see, from participating in this activity, that determination has both a personal and organizational face.

List examples from your life experiences that have called for your determination and that you, in turn, have met the challenge.

_____

_____

_____

_____

_____

We recognize that this list is *representative of your life experiences* rather than a comprehensive list.

Leadership Seminar Participant Responses:

> A high school teacher said that I wasn't college material. I showed him by graduating from the university with honors.

> A junior high school coach cut me from the basketball team. I not only played on the first five in high school and was captain and Most Valuable Player, but also played four years of college basketball.

> I received an F in French during my freshman year of college. I buckled down, repeated the course and earned a B.

> The Annual Alumni Banquet for our department at the university was going downhill fast. It had turned into a formal banquet for a few people. A group of us professors and students took a number of steps to get and keep life in this event. It was very satisfying!

> No one wanted to be on the team of professionals that prepared our organization for the accreditation team visit. I volunteered to head this committee and discovered that, although it was a lot of work, I not only helped our organization but also learned a lot myself.

Activity 9.4b

List the situations in your present work setting that have called for determination, after which you met the challenge.

_____

_____

_____

_____

_____

Leadership Seminar Participant Responses:

> We had a manager who I could only describe as mean. A small group of us decided that we would support each other in outlasting him. After five long years, he was fired. We not only were happy, but we celebrated our endurance as a group of people who cared about our organization.

I never thought I would be good in a sales position, but I took the job when it was offered. It was very difficult at first, as I was not comfortable and really had to work through my fears and anxieties. I did so well that they appointed me as sales manager. Last year I was named the new national sales manager for the company. I am so proud of my willingness to work through the difficult times.

I was reluctant to take the job when offered, as I knew that I would have to give speeches on occasion. At that time, I had it in my mind that speeches had to be formal in order to be well received. An older colleague advised me to use my informal style since it represented who I really am. I followed her advice and was happily surprised when audiences not only tolerated but seemed to enjoy what I had to say.

I was both disappointed and angry when my new principal gave me a low rating at evaluation time. I was told that I needed to be better organized, so that students would know better what to expect from me. My faculty mentor gave me some tips on how to create a more detailed syllabus and also how to make my student assignments clearer. I was surprised when students told me that they appreciated knowing what to do and when.

COMPLEMENTARY COMMENTARY

All of these examples demonstrate the importance of self-discipline as a key element in determination. When a person experiences meaning in the interest of worthwhile purposes, both the person and the organization profit. This is what we mean when we say that determination has both a personal and an organizational face.

CASE 9: Firmness of Purpose Can Take Many Forms

One of the unexpected benefits of your experience is occasional glimpses of wisdom that you simply didn't have when you began your career. As a new hire at the beginning of your career, you were introduced to the *One Life, One Career* mantra. Changes in our society, culture, and, indeed, the world have certainly challenged this idea. With these changes, you note that there is less loyalty between organizations and their employees.

You can read almost any newspaper or magazine and discover that mergers, downsizing, outsourcing, and the like have blurred many lines of distinction between organizations, parts of the country, and nations. Your own leadership position, as well as life outside of the organization for which you work, have been significantly changed by advances in technology and communication.

A television anchor has told you that, because of your leadership position, a reporter wants to conduct an interview about what sense you make of the many changes that have taken place during your career. You know from past experience with the media that you will need to focus on two or three key ideas. To introduce and try to develop more ideas will simply confuse the reporter and public.

You also know that you will need a big idea or thesis that will tie together other parts of your presentation. This is where one of your glimpses of wisdom serves you well. You decide that determination or firmness of purpose can take many forms and is an organizing concept that will give you, the reporter, and the viewing audience something to hold onto and perhaps remember for some time to come.

Authors' Recommendations

This is a wise choice on your part. The audience that experiences any kind of presentation needs a key organizing concept. It can also be important for you to think, in advance, of concrete examples of this concept, examples that will speak to the lives and experiences of the audience.

The idea that there are many ways and forms to implement your firmness of purpose accommodates the tremendous diversity that is a part of modern-day life. This diversity can overwhelm and confuse the public unless a leader's determination is rooted in morality. Knowing and articulating these moral principles brings order to the leader and public and is the basis for public discourse and debate.

SELF INVENTORY

Now that you have completed the readings and activities on "The Power of Determination," think about what you've learned and respond to the following items on a five-point scale: 1 (low) to 5 (high).

---

1. My assessment of my self-management skills.   _____

2. My assessment of my determination in reaching personal goals.   _____

3. My assessment of my determination in reaching organizational goals.   _____

4. The extent to which I value firmness of purpose or determination on the part of those with whom I work.   _____

5. My understanding of those forces earlier in my life that have influenced my views with respect to determination.   _____

6. My belief that there are many ways to reach personal goals   _____
   rather than a single, right way.

7. My belief that there are many ways to reach organizational   _____
   goals rather than a single, right way.

8. My willingness to seek other employment opportunities   _____
   when I feel that my present position is detrimental to
   my health—physical and psychological.

9. My ability to communicate determination on behalf of   _____
   organizational goals.

10. My belief that focusing energies and empowering persons   _____
    makes a difference in personal lives and the culture
    of the organization.

Note: If you are in a group setting, form discussion groups in order to share and summarize findings.

Scoring for Self Inventory

   Total the ratings and find your score in the following scale:

41–50	Superior
31–40	Above Average
21–30	Average
11–20	Below Average
0–10	Poor

SUGGESTED READINGS

Brinkley, D. (2000). *Rosa Parks.* New York: Viking.

Dunlap, D., & Schmuck, P. (1995). *Women Leading in Education.* Albany: State University of New York Press.

Estes, C. P. (1995). *Women Who Run with the Wolves: Myths and Stores of the Wild Woman Archetype.* New York: Ballantine.

Giuliani, R. (2002). *Leadership.* New York: Miramax.

Gupton, S. L., & Slick, G. A. (1996). *Highly Successful Women Administrators: The Inside Stories of How They Got There.* Thousand Oaks, CA: Corwin Press.

10

The Power of Gratitude

Dale L. Brubaker

I t was late afternoon when, tired and hungry, we pulled into the motel parking lot. After checking in and settling into our room, we walked back out to the car to go to dinner. We saw the problem immediately—a flat tire. I called our auto club, and ten minutes later a weathered man, slight of build and in his fifties, appeared. He took charge and seemed to enjoy talking while he unbolted the lug nuts, took the wheel to his truck, found the leak caused by a long screw, plugged the tire, pumped it full of air, and put it back on the car.

His hands were calloused, full of grime that could never be entirely removed. He told me he had been a truck driver until a year or so ago when it was time to settle down. He bought 12 acres of land in the country and moved into a trailer with his wife of 30 years. With great pride in his voice and countenance, he told me about his land, home, family, and ability to do his work well.

When I returned to my motel room, I shared with my wife the gratitude I felt for this man and what he did for us. I also told her what respect I had for his talents and the appreciation he expressed for a nation in which he could own his own land.

It reminded me that gratitude and a sense of connection with persons of many and diverse talents are important elements of effective leadership.

Indeed, this appreciation for different talents is the basis for building teams and creating community in any organization. The effective leader will publicly celebrate the talents and successes of others. The opposite of this is a leader's obsession with his or her own ego gratification—the drive for individual recognition at the expense of the team and community. The individual with such out-of-control drive will experience short-run success, but in the long run both the individual and the organization will suffer.

A SENSE OF CONNECTION

Nancy, our church organist, helped me see that to be grateful is to see oneself as part of something larger and more important than oneself.

Now middle aged, she had been a child prodigy, a musical genius who played the organ and piano brilliantly. I had a question in my mind for some time and had the opportunity to pose it to her after one church service: "Do you get nervous before you play or while you are playing?"

Her clearly stated answer surprised me: "I have a certain edge on before playing but I'm never too nervous to perform well. I'm an important *part* of the service, but only one of many who make the service possible—the choir, the ministers, the custodian who prepared the sanctuary, the congregation and others."

Nancy's response told me a great deal about her success. She sees herself as part of something larger and more important than herself—the service. And she celebrates her *connection* with these persons and the service itself. Nancy and others with a similar perspective have nurtured the spiritual side of their leadership. She uses her talents to help others, such as members of the choir, identify and use their talents. This is creative leadership, not simply leadership.

Nancy's leadership lesson helped me as a public speaker. I now see my contribution in a larger context. In the past, I had the mistaken impression that my speech was at the center of the organization, and that the organization's success or failure was at stake when I was on stage. Nancy's comments helped me realize that every setting has its own history and culture, and it is my privilege to be a part of this history and culture.

How many times have you had a newly appointed leader who assumed that the organization has no history or no history of any value? It reminds me of a person who arrived at our house two hours late for a party. Upon his arrival, he looked around and said, "Oh, the party just started!"

"No," I responded, "you just arrived."

A friend told me about a newly appointed CEO who came from outside his company. The CEO called the large staff together and said, "Welcome aboard!" My friend turned to the person next to him and murmured, "I thought it was our ship." The leader who acknowledges and publicly celebrates the contributions of others in the organization's history conveys a message of connectedness, humility, and gratitude that will stand him or her well in the present and future of the organization.

Implications for Leaders

Larry D. Coble

ORIENTATION

In my view, one of the finest compliments I ever received was from a colleague who told me one day that if I felt that my office was one degree too cold or too hot, the folks in charge of controlling the office environment would "bust their butts" to get it the way I wanted it. He was sincere and certainly believed that this was the case. In reflection, it is interesting to speculate about why I was perceived in a way that would result in that type of comment.

At the same time, we have all observed leaders who have taken a strong ego and overdone it to the point that they have become arrogant. They tend to drive people away—people who leave for "health reasons." Their colleagues are sick of being around an egomaniac. These leaders represent the exact opposite of what a leader is supposed to be when it comes to tapping the power of gratitude. These are leaders who start believing that they are pretty much solely responsible for their own successes, and they fail to recognize all of the help that they have received along the way. A fundamental mistake leaders of this nature make is that they also believe they are untouchable, that the rules are different for them than for everyone else. As we continue to see on the evening news, some even believe that they are above the law. By analyzing the successes and approaches of highly effective leaders, we can learn more about how to use the power of gratitude; by analyzing the failures of ineffective leaders, we can better understand what not to do.

THE POWER OF PERSUASION

How do you honestly convince those whom you are charged with leading that you are sincerely grateful for their commitment to the goals of the organization, their personal support of you as their leader, and their many efforts? The answer is as much about who you are as what you do. For example, I really do not believe that you can "fake" gratitude over any significant time period and have people believe in you. The power of gratitude starts with a philosophy toward life and leading.

One act that certainly symbolizes the philosophy of highly effective leaders is that they are not afraid to get their hands dirty. They demonstrate by their words, and *more by their actions,* that they're not above helping do any job. On many occasions I have taken off my pin-stripe suit jacket and helped the "troops" move chairs or whatever else needed moving in order to conduct a meeting that I had scheduled and would preside over. Don't be above demonstrating that you are willing to assist with anything that needs to be done. Word of your involvement and actions will travel through the organization at rapid speed.

COLLABORATION AND COLLEGIALITY

All people in organizations want to be treated with dignity and respect. This is true whether it's the custodian or someone in the executive suite. Leadership styles that are especially conducive to promoting dignity and respect are styles that are both collaborative and collegial. These styles include striving to meet organizational goals while helping subordinates meet job-related needs and satisfactions. Leaders who successfully employ these styles attempt to get employees to work *with* rather than *for* them, they value contributions over conformity, they promote self-discipline over obedience, and they use both consensus and personal judgment as decision-making strategies.

Collaborative and collegial leaders model the philosophy that all share the responsibility for organizational success and that the leader is "first among equals." These leaders believe that each person possesses vital competencies; therefore, differences among individuals, along with individual talents, are highly valued. Leadership is rotated to the individual who possesses a particular competence that is required at a given time, and conflicts are settled by open and authentic confrontation.

THE PERSONAL TOUCH

Once again the use of strong interpersonal skills is the foundation on which the power of gratitude is constructed. Begin by being friendly and open. Demonstrate your humanness. I always visited my employees on their own turf. This demonstrated that I was willing to come to them, and it automatically eliminated the mystique and the stigma that goes with the executive suite. I sent handwritten notes. I celebrated successes. I told stories throughout the organization about the accomplishments of anyone and everyone. I responded affirmatively to invitations to join in celebrations that various employees of all status levels planned for themselves. I directed the planning of celebrations for the purpose of recognizing excellence, and I showed up. In other words, appreciation for jobs well done came through a variety of formal and informal approaches. Regardless of rank or status, all employees were appreciated for their good work.

FORMAL APPROACHES FOR EXPRESSING GRATITUDE

Every good leader I have ever known used influence beyond their formal authority, first by being who they are and then by employing techniques such as those mentioned earlier. Some formal approaches, however, can be very effective in using the power and the expression of gratitude in an organizational setting. Consider the following:

- Involve staff in making decisions relative to budgets, staffing, and other critical issues.
- Keep staff informed regarding organizational issues, concerns, and procedures.
- Provide opportunities for the staff to talk to one another.
- Consult with the staff about their professional development needs and then provide it for them, along with the necessary time commitment.
- Encourage your staff to succeed and take more risks by being tolerant, understanding, and helpful when they make mistakes.
- Promote a healthy organizational climate in which the staff can enjoy their work and are recognized for their contributions.
- Focus organizational attention on exemplary work through the use of newsletters, press releases, and ceremonies.
- Ask staff for suggestions on how to improve the organization, and follow up.
- Become an outstanding listener. Set up informal meetings on a regular basis to learn how things are actually working.
- Use your formal authority to remove barriers and roadblocks to "make things happen" and make the jobs easier for your employees.

LEARNING WHAT NOT TO DO

If your words say one thing and your actions demonstrate something else, you are in for a long haul. Some things you should consider avoiding include setting up competition among your staff. Some light, healthy competition can be fun, but when it pits staff member against staff member or team against team, the organization loses, the employees lose, and you lose.

Avoid unnecessary bureaucratic procedures. The more you can do to eliminate a formal hierarchy, the better the communication; the better the communication, the better the outcomes, whether you are trying to produce products or services.

Avoid arbitrarily designed reward systems. You are not an expert on the type of rewards your employees may want. Involve them in designing a reward system that is commensurate with jobs that are performed well and that recognize team achievement as well as outstanding individual performance.

Finally, do not set unrealistic goals. Goals should require a "stretch," but they should also be attainable. Do not make the mistake of failing to provide training and technical support. Also, avoid the pitfall of limited participation of your employees. Involve them in meetings and decisions that have a direct impact on their jobs.

CONCLUSION

Your success depends in large measure on your ability to use the power of gratitude. Reflecting on all those who have helped you along the way and who have contributed to your successes is a great place to begin. Always recognize that, whatever the extent of your success, key individuals have made a difference in your accomplishments to date and will continue to do so in your future leadership roles.

Build a culture that emphasizes the good that comes from expressing gratitude for kindnesses and jobs well done. Exercise care in recognizing and appreciating contributors at all levels within the organization. As a leader, your expressions of gratitude must be sincere and well deserved. Otherwise, your expressions will have little impact. Build an organization that has a reputation as a "thank you" place.

ENGAGING SELF AND OTHERS

The following activities and materials are designed to involve you, the reader, and others, as you and they create learning communities. Because our major emphasis in this book is on leadership lessons for adults, the exercises focus on adult learning.

Activity 10.1

Do you believe that power can be realized by you and your organization through expressing gratitude to workers for good work? Provide the rationale behind your answer.

_____

_____

_____

_____

_____

_____

Activity 10.2

List some practical ways in which you can express sincere gratitude to workers who make a contribution to your organization. Some people say that compliments are sometimes appreciated more than salary raises. Do you agree?

_____

_____

_____

_____

_____

_____

Activity 10.3

Frequently, the CEO and top administrators receive most of the praise and other benefits associated with success. How do you think this gratitude could be shared with the rest of the personnel? Does the expression of gratitude really improve morale and self-worth?

_____

_____

_____

_____

_____

_____

Activity 10.4

Place a check mark next to the practices/principles that are used in your organization.

- ❑ We have an established formal procedure for recognizing and celebrating exemplary performance on the part of workers.
- ❑ Good work is recognized through informal procedures, such as writing notes and complimenting people in informal conversations.
- ❑ Individuals in "low status" as well as "high status" jobs are recognized for good work.
- ❑ Workers show appreciation for being members of your organization.
- ❑ Gratitude is expressed for the contribution made by workers who preceded the current staff.
- ❑ Expressions of gratitude are always sincere; gratitude is never expressed for poor performance.
- ❑ The organization is recognized as one that expresses gratitude for the good efforts of its workers.
- ❑ Salary raises and promotions are used as formal ways to express appreciation for a job well done.
- ❑ The proper use of expressions of gratitude in the organization makes an impact on the morale and performance of workers.

COMPLEMENTARY COMMENTARY

Gratitude, a sense of appreciation, is an attribute usually associated with a person. It can also have an organizational face, however, in that an observer notices how settings within the organization have cooperation, respect, and teamwork as norms. Once again, leaders set the tone for settings in which gratitude can thrive. We will focus on gratitude as an attitude and as an expression or action. The expression of gratitude may be verbal and/or nonverbal. Smiles and nods of approval, for example, can be as powerful as words.

Activity 10.5a

List examples from your work setting in which others expressed their gratitude to you.

_____

_____

_____

Leadership Seminar Participant Responses:

> At the beginning of our group meeting, I was thanked for writing an excellent subcommittee report. Surprisingly enough, it was a co-worker who thanked me, after which the group leader concurred.

> The new manager came on board at the very same time an accreditation work committee was being formed in order to prepare for the visit of next year's accreditation assessment team. I was surprised, almost shocked, when the new manager thanked me for the fine job I had done as the former work committee chair. At first, I thought this was a set-up in order to get me to chair the present work committee, but that wasn't it at all, because a new chair was appointed.

> I sometimes think that our company's newsletter is just another handout, but I was surprised how much I appreciated it when my colleagues brought to my attention an item about an article I had written for the local newspaper.

> I got a note from a person down the hall thanking me for helping her work out a glitch on her computer. It meant a lot to me that she took the time to do this. It was thoughtful.

> I was surprised how much I was moved by a simple comment from the sales person: "We appreciate your business."

> I began my career in a university where only one kind of research was appreciated and rewarded. I am now at a university that appreciates and rewards different kinds of research as long as they are done well.

COMPLEMENTARY COMMENTARY

All of these comments demonstrate a sense of connection between persons of many and diverse talents. In most cases, they demonstrate a public celebration of the talents and successes of others. They also emphasize that the culture was made richer by the individual's contribution. Although an individual was rewarded with an expression of gratitude, it was also made clear that the organization was enhanced by such a contribution.

Activity 10.5b

We now move to the matter of how you have shown your gratitude to others. List the ways you have done this in your organization.

_____

_____

_____

Leadership Seminar Participant Responses:

Seminar participants seemed more deliberative in responding to this exercise. One member explained this by saying, "We're not used to thinking so much about this."

This seems like a simple thing, but I greet fellow workers with a warm "Good morning," after which we usually engage in brief small talk.

I have a few colleagues that I really connect with, and we have certain common interests—usually politics or sports related. I will sometimes buy an extra copy of a bargain book that interests me and give it to him or her.

When I see an item in a newsletter or newspaper that features a contribution from a colleague that I like, I drop a note of congratulations to him or her.

I really respect people who speak well in front of groups. I usually thank them for their fine speech sometime during the day.

I am much more generous in expressing my gratitude now than I was when I began my career. My competitive nature then prompted me to play a kind of "teeter-totter" game: you go up and I go down. I now go out of my way to celebrate colleagues' victories—both verbally and in writing.

NOTE: All of the comments by participants in this section of the book convey the importance of gratitude in the individual's life, as well as the culture of the organization.

CASE 10: A Newly Appointed CEO and Friend Seeks Your Advice

A friend from graduate school has recently been named the CEO of your organization. You hadn't applied for or wanted this position because your talents are best realized as a core group member rather than as a CEO. Although you generally support this new appointment, you are naturally aware that some problems may ensue because of your previous relationship with your friend. One of the main problems will simply be that your friend will expect more of you because of your relationship. You will probably be asked to give more of your resources, time, and talents to the organization.

Shortly after the CEO appointment, your friend visits your home and asks for any advice you have with regard to the position, the culture of the organization, and the like. What do you say?

_____

_____

_____

_____

_____

Authors' Recommendations

You have experienced several new CEOs during your career and so you know how critical the CEO's first steps can be. Most of the new appointees have operated out of a deficit model. That is, their actions have focused on what is missing or wrong in the organization. You would be wise to advise your friend to give attention to what has gone right in the history and culture of the organization as well as new challenges that must be faced.

If implemented, your advice will assure members of the organization that the new CEO has a wider perspective and is not simply ego driven. The new CEO will also communicate the fact that homework has been done in order to know and understand the history and culture of the organization. A sense of connection with these matters will be enhanced by emphasizing the importance of teamwork. Implicit in this will be the idea that a "Lone Ranger" approach to leadership is unacceptable. Employees' talents will be invited and rewarded within the context of the organization's vision, mission, goals, and objectives.

Above all, the new CEO will communicate a sense of gratitude for the opportunity to lead the organization.

SELF INVENTORY

Now that you have completed the readings and activities on "The Power of Gratitude," think about what you've learned and respond to the following items on a five-point scale: 1 (low) to 5 (high).

1. My recognition that gratitude and respect for one's talents go hand in hand.	_____
2. The extent to which I feel gratitude.	_____
3. The extent to which I express gratitude in one-on-one situations.	_____
4. The extent to which I publicly express gratitude in group settings.	_____
5. The extent to which I have my ego in check.	_____
6. The extent to which I celebrate the connections between persons in the organization where I work.	_____
7. My awareness as to the possible distinction between the word "individual" and the word "person."	_____
8. The extent to which I understand the history of the organization in which I work.	_____
9. The extent to which I publicly celebrate positive aspects of this history.	_____
10. My understanding of the relationship between humility and gratitude.	_____

Note: If you are in a group setting, form discussion groups in order to share and summarize findings.

Scoring for Self Inventory
    Total the ratings and find your score in the following scale:

41–50	Superior
31–40	Above Average
21–30	Average
11–20	Below Average
0–10	Poor

SUGGESTED READINGS

Ashe, A. & Rampersad, A. (1994). *Days of Grace: A Memoir.* New York: Random House.

Hoyle, J. R. (2002). *Leadership and the Force of Love: Six Keys to Motivating with Love.* Thousand Oaks, CA: Corwin Press.

Pellicere, L. O. (2003). *Caring Enough to Lead: How Reflecting Thought Leads to Moral Leadership.* Thousand Oaks, CA: Corwin Press.

Rubin, H. (2002). *Collaborative Leadership: Developing Effective Partnerships in Communities and Schools.* Thousand Oaks, CA: Corwin Press.

11

The Power of
Private Victories

Dale L. Brubaker

Norman Garrett III, CEO of the Mazda Miata Club of America, is one of a three-person team who designed the Mazda Miata, a two-seat roadster convertible that took the country by storm. A native of Greensboro, North Carolina, and graduate of Grimsley High School, he majored in automotive engineering at Georgia Tech and graduated in 1981. Graduation was quickly followed by 13 lucrative engineering job offers. He took what appeared to be the most attractive offer. Garrett's character was tested, however, when he and several others were relieved of their jobs with this California company. He picked himself up and joined Mazda in California. While there, he was offered a challenge few automotive engineers are given—to join a three-person team that would design a two-seat sports car.

The amazing thing is that he didn't doubt for a moment that he could do it. In a March 1989 interview at the Volvo plant in North Carolina, he said: "We three knew more about how to build this kind of sports car than any other group of three people in the industry." He added, "Our challenge was to think as one person rather than as a committee."

To do so, their energy had to be focused. This ability to focus was tested when Mazda wanted to use front-wheel drive because their factories produced front-wheel drive cars. Given the history of sports cars, Garrett argued that a rear-wheel drive car would always handle better than a front-wheel drive car. He won! But not before putting time, effort, and additional research into the project over a sustained period of time.

For his good work, Garrett became known as the architect of the interior of the Miata, and his three-person team was acclaimed for bringing precision and imagination to their work.

In the 1990s, the Miata was one of the most talked-about cars on the road. *Road and Track* named it one of the five best cars in the world, along with the Ferrari Testarossa, the Porsche 911 Carrere, the Corvette ZR-1, and the Mercedes-Benz 300E. Its 1.6-liter, four-cylinder engine and its engineering fine points have been applauded by car magazine editors and sports car drivers.

One of the most interesting things Garrett and other Americans experienced while working with Japanese leaders was the interpersonal conflict in moving from the drawing boards to production. Garrett felt that the Japanese management style was "Here's your job, do it!" The Americans were never told, "You've done a good job!" Garrett said, "We Americans made all kinds of noise assuming our self-importance." The impasse between cultures became a challenge to Garrett, and he made a speech saying, "We want to contribute *and* be recognized for it."

Garrett left Mazda to work as a Senior Product Planning Analyst at Volvo GM Heavy Truck Corporation in Greensboro, after which he returned full time to the position of CEO of Mazda Miata Club of America. With time, he became aware that many, if not most, of the victories one realizes are in the personal satisfaction one experienced in achieving them. In short, they are *private victories.*

THE MEANING OF PRIVATE VICTORIES

All of us can identify with Garrett's desire for public acclaim and appreciation for good work. Successful organizations recognize this need on the part of employees and adjust their reward systems accordingly. In spite of these gestures, however, a person's efforts and expertise will never be fully known, yet alone publicly acknowledged. In fact, a person with experience and maturity recognizes that seemingly small behaviors are the mortar that holds the more dramatic bricks in place in an organization. Recognizing this is the first step in experiencing the meaning of private victories.

The second step is knowing that mastering something by harnessing your inner drive is essential. Garrett realized, in retrospect, that he had honed his skill as a tennis player by working on the practice backboard as much as he played on the tennis court itself. Most of the time when he practiced drills on the backboard, no one was there to observe his efforts. The self-determination and self-discipline he demonstrated in practicing prepared the way for improvement during tennis matches.

The same held true for his work as architect of the interior of the Miata.

The third step is being true to your own compass. As Garrett observed in 1989, "You feed your own engine. You can't let others determine your worth."

One place he learned this was when he was one of five boys who tried out for cheerleading at Grimsley High School. "We were all equally bad," he said, "but with hard work, we learned all of the Carolina stunts." He added, "We got a lot of jeering from some of the boys, but I learned to stand up for what I believed in and rely on my internal support system. I learned to draw on my own resources as well as my faith in God. If you depend only on an external support system, you're doomed to fail."

The fourth step in gaining meaning that comes from private victories is to build on the confidence you gain in order to take reasonable risks. Garrett did this by founding the Mazda Miata Club of America. "I've learned to trust myself by being prepared—having my ducks in order," he said. His heroes are people like Thomas Jefferson, Benjamin Franklin, and Thomas Edison.

The fifth and final step shared by Garrett concerns the importance of listening—particularly to the stories of his mentors and the concerns of others. His grandfather was a special mentor as well as a good listener, as were a few teachers and coaches who made a difference in his life.

When Garrett was fired by a California corporation, support groups in his church helped him see that making money was not the answer. "I discovered that rich is an adjective, not a noun," he added.

The common denominator held by those I have interviewed with regard to private victories is their belief that the way they choose to think and act makes the difference in the quality of their lives and leadership. This understanding is a gift to themselves and others—a gift that gives us hope for a better future.

Implications for Leaders

Larry D. Coble

ORIENTATION

We have already established that leaders don't learn very much from their achievements, but it is their stumbles, past mistakes, and failures that tend to shape their development. It is our achievements, however, that sustain us. Our achievements and our victories nurture us and create conditions in which we feel good about ourselves. As leaders in large, complex organizations, we are expected to have what I refer to as public victories. Public victories are those that are observed or felt throughout the organization. Such public victories come in the way of a change initiative that we have led, a new product that we have helped launch, an expanded service that we have provided, an innovation that we have introduced, a promotion for ourselves, a promotion for someone we have mentored, or any other outcome that calls attention to the good work we have done. These public victories are résumé builders. They make statements about our identity in a particular corporate setting.

Over the years, I have been fortunate to have had many public victories, and I have enjoyed them. You can't survive as a leader without them. I can tell you for a fact, however, that when you "go the distance," you will remember the public victories, but it will be the private victories that will count for the most in your mind and heart. You, and only you (and to some extent your family), will understand the commitment of time and energy and the hard decisions that went into getting buy-in to do what's right, or flying solo and shouldering all the responsibility for the eventual outcomes of your decision. Public victories make the headlines, but it is the private victories that become your on-the-job therapy.

PRIVATE VICTORIES DEFINED

Even the most successful leaders would cringe if they were aware of all the criticism and second-guessing that goes on around them regarding their leadership. The view from a position of being in charge is very different from the view of someone who is looking on and taking pot shots. Just know that, frequently when you have a public victory, your critics are not happy for you. For these reasons and many others, it is important that leaders learn to recognize and savor private victories.

Private victories have little to do with technical competence; instead, they have more to do with leadership behaviors. Private victories are those enjoyed by the leader who has called on every ounce of skill that she has to make things happen to improve herself and her organization. Getting your ego under control, remaining persistent and unwavering until a project is completed, successfully teaching your philosophy or vision to an adversary, building important coalitions, not boasting about public wins, living one day at a time but with your eyes fixed on the horizon, and not taking things too personally are examples of private victories.

TAKING CHARGE OF YOUR PRIVATE VICTORIES

If you are a leader who wants to be a perpetual learner, private victories will become increasingly important to you. Private victories are not victories over another person. Private victories are not made up of win-lose scenarios. *Private victories are victories over yourself and primarily how you choose to respond to the world around you.* As you develop to higher and higher levels, you will be competing only with yourself. This idea of competing only with yourself is a hard lesson for many to learn.

I must admit that, early in my career and even well into mid-career, I wanted to be the best, to beat someone out, to prove that I was "the man." Gradually, as I became more and more introspective, I realized that my obsession was shifting from competing with others to prove that I was a better leader than they were, to competing with myself, within my skill set and drive, to become the most effective leader that I could become. I stopped comparing my accomplishments with my contemporaries and started focusing on how I could get better without someone else having to lose. When this happened, I started doing some of the best work of my career. I was no longer focusing on a lot of "show" to better position me for that next job, but I was concentrating on how to make a lasting impact on the organization in my current role. When you get to this stage in your development, the next job will take care of itself.

Taking charge of your private victories includes analyzing your own perceptions of your successes and failures and undergoing a kind of self-performance management review. Through the reflection process, you can plan and implement future self-improvement projects. This approach will assist you in building self-confidence and will improve your morale. As you master this approach, you will become more realistic in judging your own successes.

Private victory can occur with a public loss, and there can be a public victory without a private victory. Private victories are about what is in your heart. You may lose something that is very important to you in an organizational sense, but you experience a private victory because of the personal growth that took place during the process. On the other hand, you may have a big public win, but, because there were too many casualties along the way, you may feel that you lost personally. Knowing when to step up and knowing when to step down can be private victories.

You must try to turn every situation into a learning situation. When something very good occurs or when something very bad occurs, consider using what the army calls the "after-action review." Try to understand what went on to cause the event to occur. Practice observing yourself. I often tell developing leaders that they are capable not only of participating in some of our leadership development activities, but also of observing themselves participate. This observation of self begins to open the door to being truly honest with yourself about yourself, and it sets the stage for future development and private victories.

CELEBRATING PRIVATE VICTORIES

I have talked about the importance of taking the time to savor your private victories. Once again, this does not mean boasting about your accomplishments.

This is about a victory over self. It is about saying to yourself, "I have grown as a result of this challenge, and I am a better leader and a better human being than I was before this experience." Quietly pat yourself on the back and reward yourself in a way that is right for you.

As simple as it may sound, a reward that I enjoyed very much after reflecting on a private victory was a ride in my car, usually heading home and usually late at night, with the windows and moon roof open and my car phone turned off. It was a time for me to commune with the night. It was a feeling of peacefulness after tremendous exertion of energy, much like an athlete feels after beating his own record. Watching a late night talk show and feeling "free" was another reward, as was the purchase of a new shirt or tie.

Every leader needs one or two trusted colleagues who will tell you when "the mouthwash or the deodorant is not working." These kinds of people are not only professional associates, they are your true friends as well. They will be around for you when you no longer occupy the executive suite and when you no longer control their bonuses, promotions, and general plight in the organization. I found great value in sometimes sharing my private victories with them and having them share theirs with me. We "debriefed" the private victories together. Sometimes we just sat and didn't say that much. No matter how big or how important you feel you have become, don't ever forget that leadership is a process, not an individual.

CONCLUSION

Public victories and private victories are both important. You are expected to win big with public victories. That's what you're getting paid to do. You're getting paid to leave the organization a better organization than it was when you took over. If you fail, you will not be viewed as having been an effective leader. It is within this leadership process of improving your organization, however, that the will to achieve private victories must occur. Victory over oneself is the greatest private victory. Use the feelings of personal satisfaction in private victory to encourage further risk taking and venture into the unknown. Reflect on past accomplishments to identify strategies and behaviors that will help you identify and solve future leadership challenges. Give credit to others who contribute to your private victories.

ENGAGING SELF AND OTHERS

The following activities and materials are designed to involve you, the reader, and others, as you and they create learning communities. Because our major emphasis in this book is on leadership lessons for adults, the exercises focus on adult learning.

Activity 11.1

Reflect on the successes you have had in the past. To what extent did these victories help you become a better leader in later years? Also, to what extent have you learned from experiences in which you were not as successful?

_____

_____

_____

_____

_____

Activity 11.2

List 10 adjectives that describe your feelings when reflecting on significant private victories.

1. _____

2. _____

3. _____

4. _____

5. _____

6. _____

7. _____

8. _____

9. _____

10. _____

Now list 5 adjectives that describe your feelings when you have not been as successful in an endeavor.

1. _____

2. _____

3. _____

4. _____

5. _____

Activity 11.3

Place a checkmark next to each of the following procedures/principles that you employ in your role as a leader.

- ❑ Privately give yourself credit for significant accomplishments in your work.
- ❑ Refrain from boasting about accomplishments.
- ❑ Reflect on past accomplishments to identify strategies and behaviors that can be employed to solve future problems.
- ❑ Give credit to others who contributed to your private successes.
- ❑ Reflect on past successes to enhance morale and self-worth.
- ❑ Use own perceptions of accomplishments as well as opinions of others in determining self-worth.
- ❑ Use feelings of self-worth gained through private victories to make changes and to venture into the unknown.
- ❑ Are realistic in judging own accomplishments.

COMPLEMENTARY COMMENTARY

We usually associate victories with public settings. A team victory in athletics, for example, is a victory *over* another team. Political victories, such as reaching agreement at a board meeting on an issue that the public finds important, are most often media events designed to increase the political capital of the victor. Private victories have their own intrinsic rewards.

Activity 11.4a

List some examples of private victories you have experienced in your personal life.

_____

_____

_____

_____

_____

_____

Leadership Seminar Participant Responses:

I remember many times when raising our children that I felt a special warmth toward them because of something I contributed to their development. Yet, they have never mentioned these times to me, and, in fact, they may have forgotten them. The gift to them is really a gift to myself—a memory of a good time.

I decided to give a thousand dollars to a charity that I strongly believe in, with the stipulation that the gift should be an anonymous one.

I sometimes defend a controversial friend when he is criticized. I don't tell him when this happens. I just think that the critic doesn't have a balanced view of my friend.

I've noticed that my spouse and I do a lot of good things for each other around the house without expecting recognition. When we were first married, I did expect to be thanked, but I now see this as beside the point.

Activity 11.4b

List some examples of private victories you have experienced in your workplace.

_____

_____

_____

_____

_____

_____

Leadership Seminar Participant Responses:

> I served on a committee that rewarded a colleague with a paid three months off from work for personal development. The committee didn't want to support this colleague, but I used what credibility I had to change their minds. It wasn't appropriate for me to tell my colleague about my role in this matter. My victory was a private one: a deserving colleague got the "sabbatical."

> A few months after giving a copy of a book I wrote to an administrator, he said, "What a great thing it is that Seymour Sarason from Yale University wrote a fore-word for your book!" He said nothing about the book's content.

> Other people on the committee I chaired simply didn't accept responsibility for the work that needed to be done—especially the writing of the report. I finally gave up and did the work myself. I didn't whine about it and tell others what happened. I would have, however, earlier in my career.

> I have come to accept that some of my best teaching will never be acknowledged by the students. My payoff is knowing that I really taught well. I should add that sometimes, when I don't think that I have done a good job, they compliment me on a job well done.

COMPLEMENTARY COMMENTARY

Self-determination and self-discipline are necessary in order to build an intrinsic reward system. By using one's moral compass as a guide, storms can be weathered with private victories spurring one on to do the right things and to do things right.

CASE 11: A Committee Assignment Worth Having

As a high-ranking administrator in your organization, you have had the opportunity to attend several conferences. One of the best of these professional development opportunities focused on organizational culture. The subtopic that interested you the most was titled "Extrinsic and Intrinsic Rewards." Fortunately, another leader in your organization also attended the day-long session that dealt with this subtopic and found it of interest and value.

On the flight home from the conference, the two of you talked about the fact that your organization has not given attention to the reward system presently in place and its strengths and weaknesses. In fact, it really couldn't be called a "system" because it developed informally without much attention to its overall quality.

During your conversation, your colleague said, "What we really need is a group of people or committee that will study this matter and make recommendations. This could be a major part of improving the culture of our organization." You agree and bring this to the attention of the CEO, who supports your suggestion and appoints you and your colleague as co-chairs of the committee.

Your first step is the important one of agreeing on the purpose of the committee. You know that committees frequently have little effect on the organization, and you and your colleague don't want to put time, energy, and expertise into an effort that won't make a difference. The two of you agree that the purpose of your committee is to assess the organization's present attention to extrinsic and intrinsic rewards, after which you will recommend that an overall system for giving attention to this matter will be put in place.

The first thing you discover during your assessment of current practices is that nearly all of the rewards are given to individuals, although the rhetoric of the organization emphasizes team efforts. And, there simply has been no attention given to intrinsic or private rewards. You and your friend decide to use the language you learned at the conference: private rewards are called private victories and public rewards are named public victories.

The second finding was a reinforcement of what you initially thought was true. No system or overall plan exists in place in your organization for giving attention to the importance of extrinsic and intrinsic victories. What is in place simply evolved without attention to overall structure. As a result, the place of a reward subsystem within the larger conceptual framework called "the culture of the organization" was not discussed. Using the language of Senge in *The Fifth Discipline*, a mental model was missing.

You and your convention colleague form a five-person committee, which agrees that attention to this mental model idea is essential and that the committee's basic assumptions about the value of an extrinsic and intrinsic reward system must be clearly spelled out at the onset of your efforts.

The first assumption that all committee members agree on, after a good deal of discussion, is that although all private victories won't be publicly acknowledged, the organization must make a greater effort to make private victories public.

The second assumption agreed on by the committee is that public rewards must be team oriented, where possible, in order to be consistent with organizational rhetoric emphasizing teamwork and team accomplishments.

Your committee continues its deliberations and agrees that specific strategies for implementing committee recommendations will be dealt with only after the committee has had sufficient time to discuss particular aspects of the mental model that needs to be constructed.

How do you feel about progress made to date, and what do you envision as the next steps as co-chair of the committee?

_____

_____

_____

_____

_____

_____

Authors' Recommendations

You certainly seem to be on track and are wise to construct a mental model that will be the map for further committee actions. If you had failed to follow this overall committee plan, you would have fallen into the same pattern that had evolved in the organization: piecemeal efforts would be made at the expense of a more encompassing approach to the matter of extrinsic and intrinsic rewards.

As you move forward with strategies for taking your recommendations to others in the organization, it is important to consider ways in which members of the organization can experience ownership of ideas. In particular, the committee's plan must be presented as a springboard of ideas rather than a finished product.

SELF INVENTORY

Now that you have completed the readings and activities on "The Power of Private Victories," think about what you've learned and respond to the following items on a five-point scale: 1 (low) to 5 (high).

---

1. I am confident that I have the ability to focus my energy
   in order to accomplish what I consider to be a desirable purpose.   _____

2. When necessary, I have the ability to be a member of
   a group that thinks as one rather than being a committee
   with disparate views.   _____

3. I have the ability to bring precision and creativity to my work.   _____

4. Although I appreciate being publicly rewarded, I can get a
   good deal of pleasure and motivation from private victories.   _____

5. I can set aside self-importance in order to accomplish team goals.   _____

6. I can accept the fact that a person's efforts and expertise
   might never be fully known.   _____

7. I recognize and accept the fact that seemingly small
   behaviors are the mortar that holds the more dramatic
   bricks in place in an organization.   _____

8. Self-determination and self-discipline are a major part of
   my leadership style.   _____

9. My internal support system gives me the confidence to
   move forward even when others fail to support me.   _____

10. The ability to listen is an essential tool in my leadership style.   _____

Note: If you are in a group setting, form discussion groups in order to share and summarize findings.

Scoring for Self Inventory

Total the ratings and find your score in the following scale:

41–50	Superior
31–40	Above Average
21–30	Average
11–20	Below Average
0–10	Poor

SUGGESTED READINGS

Bollman, L. G. & Deal, T. E. (2002). *Reframing the Path to School Leadership: A Guide for Teachers and Principals.* Thousand Oaks, CA: Corwin Press.

Cashman, K. (2003). *Awakening the Leader Within: A Story of Transformation.* Hoboken, NJ: Wiley.

Haslett, B., Geis, F. L., & Carter, M. R. (1992). *The Organizational Woman: Power and Paradox.* Norwood, NJ: Ablex.

Podesta, C., & Sanderson, V. (1999). *Life Would Be Easy If It Weren't for Other People.* Thousand Oaks, CA: Corwin Press.

12

The Power of
Your Moral Compass

Dale L. Brubaker

Probably no object represents a sense of direction more than a compass. As children, many of us found the compass magical in helping us find our way when we were lost. Organizations also get lost and have to find their way out of the woods. In recent years, a good deal of attention has been given to organizational vision. We would also do well to talk about the leader's personal vision. The leader's moral compass is a guide that influences the behavior of others in the organization.

In following your moral compass, there are times when you will feel like you are in exile. Your opposition to mainstream thinking and acting will separate you from the majority of people in your organization who desire certain things you don't think the organization needs or should have. For example, a school superintendent may be pressured by a majority of citizens and some special interest groups to resegregate the schools in the school system. Your loyal opposition may seem more opposing than loyal.

Certain reminders may be helpful in getting through these rough times:

• First, what you do as a leader is a living testament that influences others. Mission statements and other written documents pale in significance to a lived sense of direction—your moral vision in action. Erving Goffman, author of the classic work *The Presentation of Self in Everyday Life*, argues that there is no substitute for authenticity. People may criticize you for your position, but they probably won't criticize you for being deceitful. In the process, you will receive support from some people you didn't expect to be in your camp. Knowing what you believe and acting on it will keep you from muddling along and affirming contradictory aspects inherent in any leader's work.

• Second, people will best understand your moral vision if you have an overall story of the journey you think the organization should take. Specific details have little meaning unless they are part of a larger picture, and this picture tends to be remembered when part of a narrative.

The story comes to life when the leader shares ways in which he or she has learned from situations similar to those challenging the organization. For example, the story of how an organization can be enriched by diversity can come to life when the leader points out that our forebears were in some sense aliens living in exile when they came to our country's shores. The challenge was to find ways in which they could be integrated into mainstream culture while still appreciating their heritage. Examples from the leader's family, describing where opportunities were afforded and taken advantage of, can also bring life to the story.

• Third, feed your strengths and starve your weaknesses when engaged in a controversial situation that makes you feel excluded or in exile. If you are an expert networker, use this informal style to your advantage. If you are an accomplished speaker in more formal settings, use this to your advantage. In both cases, your energy and commitment will be conveyed. As you convey this, you teach others, and the best way to learn is to teach. An honest assessment of your strengths and weaknesses is essential. A trusted colleague or core group can be an important part of your self-assessment. A prominent CEO shared this insight: "When I began my career, I was insecure and thought too much about those things I didn't do well. With time and experience, I used and celebrated my assets more."

• Fourth, the wise leader recognizes that leader growth usually occurs when we experience pain and discomfort. It is during these challenging times that real learning occurs. You are forced to examine who you are in relation to the challenge faced and you'll often discover talents you didn't know you had.

A CEO shared sthe following during an interview: "After many years, I've learned that my spiritual growth consists in large measure of nurturing myself amidst political realities. Survival is staying afloat while still being mindful that the center of control is external. With nurturing, the focus of control is internal."

• Fifth, knowing the difference between coping and changing can help you draw a map for your personal and professional future. To cope is to use short-range survival techniques such as increased physical exercise, some kinds of therapy, and prescription drugs. Change, however, involves altering some habits and routines that move you out of your comfort zones. It may even mean leaving the setting for a new job or career.

Mother Teresa was a person who lived in a kind of self-imposed exile as she reached out to the sick and poor in the slums of Calcutta, India. It was a kind of self-imposed exile in that she rejected most of the technological advances of modern society. Some of those who joined her in her work were initially critical of her rejection of modernity—for example, her insistence that clothes be washed by hand, rather than in a washing machine. Most of these critics, however, came to see that they had to experience what the down-and-out experienced in order to be compassionate leaders.

The simplicity of Mother Teresa's words of love and advocacy for those less fortunate were at the heart of her spirituality. Her sense of humor was also evident in her interpersonal relationships, while at the same time not detracting from her moral principles. Although she wrote nothing for publication, her speeches were recorded by José Luis González-Balado, a Spanish journalist. These inspiring words, short quotes, stories, prayers, as well as 15 black-and-white photographs of Mother Teresa are collected in a book titled *Mother Teresa: In My Own Words,* included in the Suggested Readings at the end of this chapter.

In conclusion, periods of exile as a leader caused by your willingness to follow your moral compass are usually painful, but they can lead to renewal that will stand you well in the long run. You will be living the lessons we learned as children in religious and educational organizations. In a sense, we will become our own heroes—the mark of a leader who has a moral compass.

Implications for Leaders

Larry D. Coble

ORIENTATION

The idea of the power of the moral compass for leaders is more far reaching than our traditional views of morality. From my perspective, the axis on which the leader's moral compass spins is the leader's core values, the "deep stuff" of his or her make-up. Many would refer to this as executive character. Leaders must know the line that they will absolutely not cross.

Those around them constantly observe leaders all the time. How they dress, how they speak to others, the meetings they attend, the meetings from which they are absent, and the respect that they show for people who can't help them advance are just a few examples of what the "leader watchers" are tuned in to. If leaders are in a formal role, they're on stage, and the higher they are in the organization, the more people are in attendance for the performance. Understand that a leader's behavior, whether perceived to be positive or negative, sets examples for those in the organization who are watching.

Many leaders significantly underestimate the importance of serving as a role model for the organization. People are observing everything you do that can be observed, and they interpret your behavior as if you had telegraphed a message. The messages you send, whether intended or not, will be viewed under the microscope of ethical behavior, and they will be interpreted as a reading on your moral compass.

COMPONENTS OF A MORAL CULTURE

The leader's core values set the tone for the organization. It is easy to see how the personality of the leader in charge and other subordinate leaders influence the day-to-day climate of the organization and certainly the overall culture. Whatever your core values are—and I would advise some real soul searching here—lead by officially adopting and promoting a set of core values for all employees. Strive to create an organizational culture that encourages employees to behave honorably and decently in all their dealings with their co-workers and customers or clients. Adopt a zero-tolerance policy for unethical behavior. Provide training that emphasizes ethical decision making and set the example that will encourage others to become exemplary citizens.

In order to help you better understand and apply the concepts of a leader's moral compass and ethical behavior, we need a structure that allows us to understand the implications for leaders. In order to apply the practice of using a moral compass, I have borrowed the results of a survey cited in a monograph, *Making Ethical Decisions* (1991), by Michael Josephson. The work reports that "thousands of people" listed the following characteristics of the most ethical person they know: honesty, integrity, promise-keeping, loyalty/fidelity, fairness, concern for others, respect for others, law-abidingness/civic duty, pursuit of excellence, and personal accountability. A wonderful way of thinking about your moral compass is to think about each of these core values as being your guide to long-term success as a leader.

HONESTY

During my career I have worked with leaders whose tongues would have fallen onto the floor if they had told a lie. I have also worked with pathological liars who didn't know the truth from a lie. These are scary people. As a leader you must never intentionally lie or misrepresent information. It is easy enough as it is to be misunderstood. My practice when communicating sensitive information was to have people state back to me what I had communicated, what their interpretation was, and what they understood the implications to be. This approach makes it easier to be viewed as being honest. It also sends the message that you want to be understood and that you care enough about your colleagues to make certain they do, in fact, understand.

Let me quickly add that, as leader, you will frequently be the caretaker of confidential information. If someone asks you about something that is confidential, simply say that it is confidential and why it is inappropriate for you to share the information. Withholding confidential information is not in any way being dishonest.

INTEGRITY AND THE LEADER'S MORAL COMPASS

Integrity, to me, means that the leader's words and actions are aligned. For most of our lives, we have heard that "actions speak louder than words." Integrity is about doing what you say you're going to do. Leaders who say one thing and do another will be looked at as leaders who lack integrity. When you are viewed as lacking in integrity, the people in your organization will not have confidence in your ability to lead them. The job of leading is impossible unless your followers have confidence in your abilities.

Honoring the "best" of your organization is an act of integrity. Leaders who find everything wrong with their department, division, hospital, school, or corporation will have their motives immediately questioned. If your organization is an unhealthy place and lacks a commitment to doing what's right, an act of integrity would be to choose to leave. In order to maintain my integrity, twice in my career I felt I had to sever my relationship with the organizations with whom I was working.

On one occasion I was asked by the board to institute a major initiative that went against my core values and belief system. I had just been granted a lucrative contract renewal but decided to leave for a position that paid less and had fewer perks, but I left with my integrity in tact. On a second occasion, I was asked to sign an ethics statement that I simply could not honor. Essentially, it asked me to guarantee that I would sever all personal friendships and any potential conflicts of interests with the organization's clients. I was a close personal friend with some of the clients, however, and the agreement I had when I was hired was that I could build a client base for private consulting. To make matters worse, I knew firsthand of many who were signing the statement and had no intention of honoring it. The decision to leave that organization was one of the best, if not the best, professional decision I ever made.

PROMISE KEEPING

Promise keeping is closely related to integrity. You cannot be a person of integrity unless you keep your promises. The "leader watchers" in your organization will quickly learn if you are a person who can be counted on to keep your promises. If you are viewed as such a person, then your colleagues will see you as being trustworthy.

On occasion, you will make a promise and circumstances will change. You will have a very good reason to abandon the promise you've made. Don't do it. Don't do it, even though keeping the promise may not be the best thing for you as the formal leader. It may not even be the absolute best thing for the organization. However, a certain expectation developed around your promise. If you go another way, the damage done by not fulfilling the commitment you made will do more harm than changing your direction based on the new information. As my grandmother would say, "You've made your bed, so now you have to lie in it."

There may be a time when you have made a promise and unanticipated consequences make it absolutely impossible for you to fulfill it. Go public with what has occurred. Explain your reasons in explicit terms. Admit that you made a mistake. Apologize for not being able to keep your promise. Ask all stakeholders to continue to support your efforts. If your track record has been one of keeping your promises, no serious harm will be done.

Keeping your promises is a visible expression that you care about the people you lead. That's what they're most interested in.

LOYALTY

Loyalty, in the leadership sense, has to do with being loyal to the organization you serve and loyal to the people with whom you work. This may sound like the same thing, but it's not. Loyalty to your organization has to do with taking pride in working for your particular organization. It is your corporate responsibility. Whoever you are as a leader and whatever you stand for is a part of your organization's corporate identity. If you're a leader and you "bad mouth" the organization for which you work, you're actually bad-mouthing yourself. If what you value begins to run counter with what the organization values, get out. Get out if you can no longer be loyal to your organization.

Loyalty to the individuals with whom you work has to do with an allegiance to them resulting from your common affiliation with the same organization. It's like being a member of the same club or the same athletic team. As a leader, you grant them loyalty before they've earned it. Create an expectation of loyalty and camaraderie for one another.

FAIRNESS

A sure-fire way to kill the spirit of those whom you lead is to project that you are playing favorites. Leaders who play favorites have a different set of standards and expectations for those considered their "pets," and then everyone else in the organization considers the leader to be unfair. You cannot afford to be considered anything but fair as a leader.

You should demonstrate that you are fair by being consistent and predictable in your actions. Your employees want to be able to predict how you will behave in practically every situation. This predictability, over time, will assist in reinforcing the perception that you are fair, assuming that your behavior demonstrates impartiality.

Leaders who are fair demonstrate equitable treatment for all of their employees. My first act as leader in one organization was to have the reserved parking spaces for the executive staff eliminated. This was an interesting experience. The "reserved" markings were painted on cement and had to be sandblasted off. Once this was completed, I announced that parking was to become open, on a first-come-first-served basis. The first to arrive got the parking space of choice. In a wonderful demonstration of exactly how it was supposed to work, the custodian, who was the first to arrive, took my old space on the first day of open parking. I loved it, and my point of fairness was punctuated.

Another way of demonstrating that you are fair is to show that you are open minded and will seek diverse points of view. This also demonstrates respect and concern for each individual.

CONCERN FOR OTHERS

Your employees bring their individual needs with them when they show up for work. Too many leaders tend to focus too much on what employees can do for the organization and too little on what the organization can do for their employees in helping meet their individual needs. The best leaders I've ever known are deeply caring and concerned about all of their employees. They use the power of their executive office to make life better for those under their direction.

Sometimes it means requesting a donation of sick leave to help an hourly employee make ends meet when his or her sick leave is used up. Sometimes it means intervening when someone has been mistreated by a boss. Sometimes it's something as simple as sending birthday cards. Whatever the situation, if you are perceived to be a caring, concerned, and compassionate leader, you will have the support you need when you need it.

RESPECT FOR OTHERS

Unless you value the humanness of every person in your organization, you need to check your moral compass. Respecting each and every individual, whether the CEO or the custodian, will ensure that you will treat him or her with dignity. Every person in your organization deserves your respect as a human being. That goes for those who disagree with your decisions as well.

When you respect the people in your organization, your leadership approach will consist of a style that makes them want to follow your direction. You will project a style that will enable them to feel that they are working "with" you and not just "for" you. Always treat others with courtesy. Even controversial decisions that impact negatively on individuals can still be handled in a manner that preserves the individuals' self-worth.

You should note that, even under the best leadership, some people at some time will believe that you are not being respectful. This usually happens with bad news that directly impacts them. It's okay. It goes with the territory.

LAW ABIDINGNESS/CIVIC DUTY

Because you have been one of the fortunate people in this world to possess a skill set and experience developmental opportunities that have thrust you into a leadership role, the stakes are higher for you. When it comes to abiding by the law, if your behavior is questioned, it is highly likely that the burden will be on you to prove your innocence. In every organization I have led, I always told my staff "if they want me, they can get me." What I meant is that, in large complex organizations, so much that goes on is out of the direct control of the formal leader. Plenty is going on in every organization that is legally questionable. Don't make it worse by willingly disobeying the law. It is a certain derailment factor that carries with it the legal consequences of such an act.

Your civic responsibility means that you are responsible civically, at least to your community. The stakes go up as you climb the leadership ladder. Decide *now* that you will support and participate in a service capacity for such organizations as the United Way, the American Cancer Society, the YMCA, the YWCA, the Boy Scouts of America, the Girl Scouts of America, and the United Arts Council, just to mention a very few. It is a given fact that you will be an active member of at least one civic club. Attend the meetings and work on the projects. That is what leaders do in fulfilling their civic responsibility.

PURSUIT OF EXCELLENCE

When it comes to leading, being average won't do much for you, the people you are leading, or the organization you are serving. Highly effective leaders are in the constant pursuit of *excellence*. I am reminded of being the kind of leader who is always just a little dissatisfied with the status quo. The style that worked for me, and I believe will work for you, is to stay involved. Set high but attainable goals, always striving for excellence through the improvement of individual performance, most especially your own, and the improvement of the organization.

The pursuit of excellence involves careful preparation and perseverance. The pursuit of excellence is not a "winging it" activity. There are few shortcuts to the pursuit of excellence. You have to want it enough in your heart to be willing to do whatever is necessary to get better and better. The pursuit does not come without sacrifice. Some people believe that you can have it all, a great organization, a wonderful home life, time for your children, and time for yourself. I don't happen to subscribe to that belief. You can't build a world-class organization, or be the best at anything, in 40 hours a week.

I used to work an average of 60 hours a week outside my home. I would leave for work many mornings when my children were still in bed, and they would be in bed asleep for the evening when I returned. I can remember, as if it were yesterday, looking at them sleeping and then moving on. When I was home, the phone calls frequently came from other executives. I was never able to completely put the work behind me and stay in the moment for very long. That also includes vacations. If this scares you, it should. If you pursue excellence in leading an organization, you will have similar experiences. My family put up with more than they should have.

PERSONAL ACCOUNTABILITY

In healthy organizations, employees accept a personal accountability for the roles they play in contributing to excellence and high productivity. First among those who must accept personal accountability is the formal leader. This is true for every level in the organization.

Based on years of experience, my advice to you as a leader is simple. When things are going well, give the credit to others. When things aren't going well, you shoulder the responsibility. Be the first to openly admit your mistakes and learn from them. This is personal accountability by example.

My belief is that much of the success and support I enjoyed over the years was due to a willingness to accept responsibility for our organizational failures and give others credit for our successes. If your people believe that you will support them when they've tried to do what's right and have come up short, they will continue to take risks that will benefit the organization. If you slap their hands and blame them for things that are ultimately your responsibility, you will completely stifle creativity and risk taking.

THE SPIRITUAL JOURNEY AND LEADERSHIP

I have a deep and abiding belief that, in the absence of a spiritual journey, you will reach a point in your personal development and then you will stall. By stall, I mean that you just will not get remarkably more effective. You may not realize what's going on, but you will find yourself continuing to use the same skill set over and over. Your challenges will begin to take on a kind of sameness; you will feel that you aren't growing and that something just isn't quite right. Some would refer to this condition as being unfulfilled.

What I am referring to, as a spiritual journey, has to do with the leader's on-going examination of her inner world. The spiritual journey is different than the practice of religion. For a leader to be on a spiritual journey is to regularly go deep within herself, always striving for understanding and new ways of making her life one that is at peace with the universe. Leaders on the journey function at higher levels than leaders who are not, and through strategies they have developed they solve problems with less effort. They recognize their connection with all of God's creations. They become less judgmental. They recognize with gratitude that there is a source in the universe that is always available to them for guidance, and they learn how to access this source that, in our culture, we refer to as God. These leaders have a general attitude of being grateful for all the abundance that has come their way.

I have been on a spiritual journey for many years and find the experience to be a major source of strength for me. The journey is not always easy because of the detractors of busy living that go on outside the leader and constantly beg for his attention. With my personality and the high need to achieve, staying on the journey can be a challenge. However, those with high needs for achievements, who choose the spiritual path, become more productive than ever. An analogy would be to consider what happens with a car when you put it into overdrive. The vehicle performs at a high level, but there is less wear and tear and effort. The same thing happens with leaders. They can produce more and more with less effort. It is my experience that this experience is much more likely to occur in mid-life. This is not an absolute, but as an old friend of mine once said, "For some things to happen, you just have to live awhile." I would also mention what I consider to be very important early in most leaders' careers: it is critical that they spend more time doing than being. Doing with great competence seems to be a prerequisite to one's early success as a leader.

If you're on the spiritual path, then good for you. If not, you should begin learning more about how to get on it. Read about spirituality and, most important, learn how to be still. When your challenges are "eating you alive," find a quiet space and be still. For me, it has and continues to be an early morning drive with a good cup of coffee. I choose a quiet mind and let whatever wants to enter enter. Don't force anything, but surrender to the process.

CONCLUSION

Tapping the power of your moral compass will be a way of guaranteeing that you are being true to yourself and the people you lead. Using this power means that you must *act*. You can talk the talk and you can commit volumes of your philosophy to writing, but unless you live out what you believe, you are a fake. Don't ever cross the line to keep a job, get a promotion, or advance selfish personal interests of any kind. Most of the time, this type of behavior will eventually catch up with you, and your career will stall or stop. If you are, tempted to cross the line, it is time to do more self-examination. Take an inventory of the standards that you are employing in your decision-making. Understand what is going on with you that would cause you to make decisions that would not contribute to the welfare of your employees, customers, or clients. You, like the rest of us, tend to judge yourself by your most noble or virtuous behavior. The rest of the world will judge you on the worst thing that you did most recently. Make sure that your moral compass points true north.

ENGAGING SELF AND OTHERS

The following activities and materials are designed to involve you, the reader, and others, as you and they create learning communities. Because our major emphasis in this book is on leadership lessons for adults, the exercises focus on adult learning.

Activity 12.1

List five behaviors that you believe should be included in a zero-tolerance policy for your organization. For one behavior, indicate the "punishment" that would be meted out for violating that policy.

_____

_____

_____

_____

_____

Activity 12.2

Currently, unethical behavior abounds within major industries in the United States. As a leader, what steps do you think you can take to assure your organization will be guided by a moral compass? Be specific.

_____

_____

_____

_____

_____

Activity 12.3

Place a checkmark next to each of the following procedures/principles that you employ in your role as a leader.

- ❑ Adopt a zero tolerance for unethical behavior.
- ❑ Provide training that emphasizes ethical values and behaviors.
- ❑ Adopt, disseminate, and promote a core list of values for your organization.
- ❑ Reflect on past experiences to provide a moral compass for the future.
- ❑ Become involved in spiritual activities.
- ❑ Strive to develop an organizational culture that encourages employees to become honorable and decent.
- ❑ Provide training concerning the value of developing and following a moral compass.
- ❑ Evaluate policies and procedures to determine whether they conform to high moral standards.
- ❑ Make decisions that are in the best interest of and contribute to the betterment of workers and clients.

Activity 12.4a

The end of the twentieth century and the beginning of the new century were marked by media accounts of leaders and organizations lacking a moral compass. The credibility of many critics was eroded when it was discovered that they had been involved in their own moral crises at some time in their careers.

List the leaders in the public eye, past and present, whom you respect for their moral compass, followed by the reason why you respect each leader.

_____

_____

_____

_____

_____

_____

Leadership Seminar Participant Responses:

Mother Teresa—Her willingness to suffer under the conditions of those she gave all of her resources and talents to help.

Mahatma Gandhi—His standing up for what he believed was right even to the point of sacrificing his life.

Martin Luther King Jr.—He gave up the comfortable life he originally had in order to change society.

Harry Truman—He told it like it was and pushed ahead even when nobody gave him a chance to win the presidential election.

Winston Churchill—He overcame defeat after defeat in order to make a major difference in the Allies winning World War II.

Activity 12.4b

Although all of these persons have their critics and were in some sense flawed human beings, they were widely respected for being living testaments in behalf of important moral values. They lived according to their moral compasses.

List the names of people in organizations where you have worked whom you respect for following their moral compasses followed by the reasons for your choices.

_____

_____

_____

_____

_____

_____

_____

Leadership Seminar Participant Responses:

Our superintendent of schools could have easily re-segregated the schools given the composition of the newly elected school board. He did what he could and used his political capital to avoid such re-segregation as long as possible. This took courage!

Our CEO has had a long record of civic participation. He has served on and been director of several boards, and in this role, has improved the lives of all within the community—especially those with the greatest needs. Perhaps most importantly, he has done this quietly without fanfare.

I especially admire our vice president for her leadership in building houses for those who could not ordinarily build them. She has used her organizational and motivational talents to involve most of the people in our organization. She is the kind of person you can't say "no" to, and once you are involved, you just feel better about yourself.

COMPLEMENTARY COMMENTARY

When we follow our moral compass, we discover that we have to give in order to get, and in the process we learn that we receive in ways that we could never imagine. Pain, and even suffering, is often involved in accomplishing worthwhile moral goals, and it is by working through these difficulties that we often experience our greatest growth and learn to get behind the eyes of those who have been in similar situations.

Activity 12.5

Seminar respondents frequently cite the challenge they face in nurturing their spiritual growth. Their busy world at work seems to consume them, thus making it difficult to find the time and space to give attention to spiritual matters.

List some of the ways that you have discovered to give attention to the spiritual side of your life.

_____

_____

_____

_____

_____

Leadership Seminar Participant Responses:

> There is a hill above my workplace, and I frequently drive to the top of it a half hour or even an hour before the workday begins. I use this time to get my mind clear so that my priorities for the day and in my life are clear.

> I make it a practice to read a book or more each month—books that are usually not directly related to my job. This helps me see the larger world out there.

> A few friends and I have identified a number of books that focus on the spiritual life. We've formed an informal book club that meets at one of our houses each month.

> I have been an active member of my church since I was a child. The stillness, singing, and sharing during our weekly service really helps me get life in perspective. And, I have, in recent years, served on some church committees that have taught me more about the organization of our denomination. Last summer, I was elected to represent our church at our state conference. It was an inspiration to be part of the singing and sharing of ideas that took place.

> Although our CEO is a member of a religious organization different from mine, it is evident in many of his meetings and other business activities that he is a spiritual person. As a result, the tone of our business culture has a spiritual quality.

COMPLEMENTARY COMMENTARY

This activity brings to our attention that work in itself is not enough. Women and men in organizations frequently discover their need to reach out spiritually in order to find meaning in their lives on a daily basis.

CASE 12: The Personal Reflection Challenge

You have struggled at times with the idea of taking or making time for personal reflection. You know that this is not a matter facing you alone. For example, you saw a program on public television in which five middle-aged leaders talked about crises in their lives and how they dealt with them. One person, a former CEO for Columbia Pictures, said that he left his job and went to a cabin to reflect for several months on where he had been in his life, where he is, and where he might go in the future. As he thinks back on this experience, he said that he probably made a mistake in isolating himself. Rather, he has decided he needed to embrace who he has become and move forward with his life.

All of this makes clear the importance of personal reflection in relation to action "on the firing line" at work. You are also aware that much of your personal reflection leads you back to the moral values that you were introduced to as a child and the moral value system that has evolved since that time.

The question that guides your thinking at this time is, "Where do I go from here with regard to personal reflection and my moral compass?"

_____

_____

_____

_____

_____

_____

Authors' Recommendations

You are right on target with your question. We believe that all of the leadership seminars in the world can't answer this question for you. Others can give you advice but *your* moral compass and *your* decision with regard to the role of personal reflection in your life and career are precisely that. We also believe that nothing is more important to your leadership decisions than your personal value system. This is precisely why we subtitled this book "Leadership Lessons on the Potential Within."

The technical decisions you make at work are relatively easy compared to the deeper question you have asked. We quickly add that your answer to this question may well vary from one time in your career to another. For example, during the beginning stage of your career you may be so involved in day-to-day decision making that you will give little attention to the matter of personal reflection. It often takes difficult challenges in your personal life to bring you back to the content of your question.

What others have done in answer to your question will be visible in the stories or narratives they share with you. We urge you to be attentive to such narratives as they are often the source of much wisdom. These stories usually share the pain and suffering of their authors. It can be helpful to you to know that you are not the only one who has experienced such pain. Finally, the distinction between coping and changing may be of special value to you as you consider short-term survival efforts in relation to longer-term changes in your work, career, and life.

SELF INVENTORY

Now that you have completed the readings and activities on "The Power of Your Moral Compass," think about what you've learned and respond to the following items on a five-point scale: 1 (low) to 5 (high).

1. As a leader, I have created a personal vision that serves as my moral _____ compass.

2. I am able to articulate this personal vision in order to influence _____ others in my organization.

3. On occasion, my opposition to mainstream thinking and acting _____ separates me from the majority of people in my organization.

4. I can live with the feeling that I am somewhat "in exile" _____ on such occasions.

5. I believe that there is no substitute for authenticity in relating _____ to self and others in the organization.

6. I am rarely, if ever, criticized for being deceitful at work. _____

7. I recognize that there are some contradictory aspects to any _____ person's work, but I do my best to minimize such contradictions.

8. I am able to illustrate my moral vision by telling the overall story _____ of the journey my organization should take.

9. I celebrate my assets more than I dwell on my weaknesses. _____

10. I have learned how to nurture my spiritual growth and know _____ the difference between coping and changing.

Note: If you are in a group setting, form discussion groups in order to share and summarize findings.

Scoring for Self Inventory
   Total the ratings and find your score in the following scale:

41–50	Superior
31–40	Above Average
21–30	Average
11–20	Below Average
0–10	Poor

SUGGESTED READINGS

Aspy, C., & Sandhu, D. (1999). *Empowering Women for Equity: A Counseling Approach.* Alexandria, VA: American Counseling Association.

Fullan, M. (2003). *The Moral Imperative of School Leadership.* Thousand Oaks, CA: Corwin Press.

Harding, S. (1991). *Whose Science? Whose Knowledge? Thinking from Women's Lives.* New York: Cornell University Press.

Sergiovanni, T. (1992). *Moral Leadership: Getting to the Heart of School Improvement.* San Francisco: Jossey-Bass.

13

The Power of Coaching and Mentoring

Dale L. Brubaker

R obert Teeter—CEO of The Coldwater Corporation, a consulting firm that conducts policy analysis and development, strategic planning, and public opinion analysis—was the senior advisor to George Herbert Walker Bush's presidential campaigns in 1988 and 1992. He was part of G-6, the half-dozen people who helped candidate Bush make key campaign decisions. After President Bush's election in 1988, Teeter became co-director of the transition team and was offered the position of deputy chief of staff and counselor to the president in the White House.

Teeter's childhood fascination with sports fit with his father's political interests in Coldwater, Michigan. Teamwork and the desire to win are essential to both athletics and politics. It was the *coaching* aspect of athletics that appealed to Teeter. From 1961 to 1963, he assisted Albion College coach Morley Fraser, whose football teams won 15 straight games, Albion's longest winning streak. Fraser knew which opponents could be trapped and which secondary defenders could be beaten deep or by action passes. He was especially good at recognizing opponents who were out of condition late in the game.

In baseball, Teeter kept graphs on opposing batters and identified opposing pitchers' tendencies that Albion's batters could exploit. Morley Fraser said, "Everything was a science to Teeter, which helped us get the edge." He added, "Bob was always enthusiastic and a tireless worker."[1]

Fraser was impressed by Teeter's ability to focus his energy and his belief that the team would always win: "Teeter's enthusiasm for the job and confidence that we would win were contagious and helped give us the tools to win."[2] As with any good coach, whether in athletics or business organizations, Teeter's confidence came from doing his homework.

Teeter, known for his professorial manner and skilled approach to public opinion and policy issues, was criticized by some colleagues during the presidential campaigns as too slow and cautious. Teeter replied in a *New York Times*'s article in 1988: "You have to have certain fundamentals in mind and not go off chasing rabbits."[3]

Teeter's ability to focus his coaching energies was obvious during the 1976 campaign when he helped Gerald Ford pull to within a few points of Jimmy Carter. During that campaign, Teeter developed a "perceptual map," a multidimensional guide to how people see the candidate on issues and traits.

His tough but civilized style was important in the Reagan campaigns. During the 1988 Bush campaign, Teeter demonstrated a zest for contrasts. This sharpening of the differences between the candidates was the result of Teeter's use of 10 focus groups of Democrats who had voted for Ronald Reagan in 1984. He discovered their visceral reactions to key issues, which allowed the Bush campaign to "define" Dukakis, the Democratic candidate.

Democratic strategist Peter Hart, in a 1988 *New York Times*'s article, gave Teeter's self-discipline the highest compliment: "He's confident without being arrogant, and he knows how to say 'no' when something's not right. Teeter has the ability to give people bad news and won't sugarcoat the data."[4] Good coaches in business and athletics share these important qualities in working with their teams.

How do people react to Teeter's style? Dotty Lynch, a former pollster who moved to CBS, said in a *New York Times*'s article: "In a world where people are trying to elbow their way in, Teeter always finds a way to make people want his advice rather than ramming it down their throats."[5] Paul Gigot described Teeter's ability in a similar vein: "Teeter is an affable and unpretentious Midwesterner."[6] Teeter has learned what any good business leader as coach knows: positional authority, as a source of power, is like a battery—the more you use it, the less there is to draw upon in the future. Expertise in its many forms is a longer-lasting source of power that earns respect.

Those who know Teeter cite his ability to get to the root of an issue or problem while many others are dealing with its symptoms. Hedrick Smith, author of *The Power Game*, applauds Teeter for being the first pollster to see the shift of the country away from a Democratic party affiliation during the Reagan presidency. Morley Fraser, Teeter's head coach at Albion College, saw Teeter's handiwork throughout the Bush–Dukakis campaign in that Teeter knew "what to say and what not to say, what to do and what not to do." Fraser added. "In particular, Teeter was a master of the element of surprise."[7]

Perhaps Teeter's biggest challenge was in deciding not to become deputy chief of staff and counselor to President Bush in 1988. His values provided the grounding for his priority-setting decision. In a *Washington Post* interview in 1988, Teeter said: "My children are both in high school in Ann Arbor, and it would have been a bad time to uproot them. I am happy with my decision."[8] Teeter preferred to attend his teenaged children's swimming meets and hockey games rather than to go to Washington's cocktail parties. Although members of a business organization or athletic team may not agree with an effective coach's priorities, they will frequently respect such coaches for priority-setting decisions that are consistent with their value systems.

This brief portrait of Bob Teeter can be instructive to us as we draw on our coaching abilities to lead others in our work settings. We can assess our own leadership traits in relation to what we have learned from Teeter's leadership style: a high energy level; the ability to focus such energy; a strong desire to achieve; a positive attitude toward self, others, and tasks to be accomplished; self-management skills; a balance between individual effort and teamwork; the ability to get to the root of a problem while many around us are dealing with the symptoms of the problem; and a value system that is respected even by those who sometimes disagree with us. In some ways it is the ultimate compliment when someone looks at us with pride and says, "That's my coach!"

Finally, it should be noted that career coaching has become a burgeoning consulting industry. Executive coaches, often female, are hired by many corporations to address their leadership needs. Corporate leaders, usually male, often choose female executive coaches because they fit the male-perceived stereotype of being less competitive, good listeners, more caring, and the like. For a discussion of these matters and more, see Laura Berman Fortgang's book, *Take Yourself to the Top: The Secrets of America's #1 Career Coach*, listed in the Suggested Readings at the end of this chapter.

Implications for Leaders

Larry D. Coble

ORIENTATION

The highest form of leadership development is coaching, because development and mentoring are critical to your success as well. The way we prefer to use these two terms in our work with leaders is that *mentoring* is an "inside" job in which the leader as learner is matched up with an established veteran leader who understands not only the leadership challenge of the specific role occupied by the developing leader but also the technical proficiencies needed to be successful in the role.

Coaching involves pairing the developing leader with a skilled "people developer" external to the organization. The coach, because she is not a member of the leader's organization, has no supervisory or evaluation responsibilities for the developing leader. The coach is an expert in helping leaders develop to their fullest leadership potential.

I want to address the power of coaching and mentoring from two different perspectives. One perspective is from having been mentored and coached myself. The other perspective is from having served as a mentor for developing leaders in organizations where I worked, as well as having served as an executive coach to a number of leaders who wanted to achieve greater capacity for leading more effectively.

It should be mentioned that some people use these two terms interchangeably. Personally, I see the two processes quite differently. A fundamental distinction is the difference mentioned earlier. To assist with additional understanding, consider *mentoring as a process that is developmental*, but for a specific job at a specific time in your life. It has more to do with developing technical skills and, in my view, will significantly strengthen your capabilities as a manager.

Coaching will certainly improve your performance in your current leadership position. Coaching takes a more holistic approach, however. *Coaching looks at your developmental needs* not only in your current role, but also as a growing and developing human being in the game of life. Leadership development is personal development. The highest form of personal development is with a skilled coach who has mastered a coaching model that will meet the learner's needs.

WHY DO WE NEED COACHING AND MENTORING?

If we were to draw on more than 30 years of research as to how leaders develop and then attempt to reduce our findings to a formula for leadership development, one variable in our formula would be the concepts of coaching and mentoring. A careful analysis of the research on how leaders develop shows that coaching, mentoring, and networking with other leaders are important to one's development. The bottom line when it comes to mentoring is that other leaders have "walked where you walk" and they understand the nature of your challenges. They are viewed to be highly effective in jobs similar to the one you're in. Learn about the successful things they're doing. Learn about their past mistakes. Listen to their advice. You can benefit from their wise counsel in understanding how they do it.

It is critical, from time to time, especially as you move into a brand new job, that you work with a mentor for the purpose of enhancing your performance. You should also definitely serve as a mentor for other developing leaders in your organization. Either way, you get the advantage of having a growth experience.

Coaching, or "executive coaching," is much less commonplace than mentoring because it requires a significantly greater commitment of time, energy, and financial resources. Coaching is a more formal process in which the coach, over time, will in all likelihood become a trusted friend who will tell you the truth about yourself. She or he will have created or adapted a coaching model that is tried and tested. The coach will use an approach that will help you become a better human being and a better leader.

THE POWER OF COACHING

A few years ago, as a follow-up to a multi-day leadership development program I had conducted, I was asked to become an executive coach for several high-ranking leaders in a single organization. Coaching is hard work, but it is important work; because of my professional relationship and personal friendship with the head of the organization that was doing the asking, I accepted. What I am about to share with you is not intended to be self-serving, but instead it illustrates for you firsthand the power of coaching.

Specifically, I was the last stop for one of these high-ranking leaders for whom I was asked to coach. By "last stop," I mean that this leader, whom we'll call Joe, was going to be terminated if I could not make a serious intervention and help him. Jumping to the end of the story, approximately nine months after the coaching began, Joe came to be recognized by the boss as the most effective of these high-ranking leaders. This was the same boss who was ready to terminate Joe and who had decided to make one last effort of assistance. There are too many factors to mention here, but let it suffice to mention that the power of coaching can be a very strong force in one's development.

Coaching depends on creating a connection with the person being coached. Ideally, this affinity occurs early in the process, but in many cases it takes time for this to emerge. Not coming across as too serious can be achieved with appropriate humor. Sharing stories of how coaches have helped you can be effective as long as you are not patronizing. As a result of all this, the person being coached both respects and likes the coach.

A MODEL FOR COACHING

There are many different coaching models and derivatives of models. The model we use came about through discussions with other seasoned coaches and our own experiences in developing leaders. Our model consists of four phases.

- *Phase 1 provides extensive feedback* to the learner using a battery of assessment instruments to capture the learner's self-perception. Included also in Phase 1 is 360-degree feedback in which the leader as learner has an opportunity to see how he is perceived by his boss, peers, and direct reports compared to his own perceptions around researched based leadership competencies. The perceptual gaps that exist provide wonderful direction in planning for self-improvement.

Phase 1 may also be enhanced through the collection of additional information from superiors, co-workers, and family members through the use of a questionnaire and interview, with feedback being provided to the leader in a format that protects the privacy of feedback sources.

- In *Phase 2, an analysis of the 360-degree feedback is conducted to identify "critical performance gaps."* The coach and the leader as learner do this analysis collaboratively. The "gaps" are then prioritized based on judgments about which must be addressed immediately, those that must be dealt with in a few months, and those that are important but not immediately critical.

- *Phase 3 of the process provides for a personal development plan* jointly developed by the coach and the leader. The development plan will prescribe the results to be achieved, the timelines for their achievement, behaviors to be modified or learned, and activities and experiences designed to modify or teach those behaviors.

- *Phase 4 will involve the actual coaching of the leader by the executive coach.* Such coaching will include clarification of results expected by superiors, subordinates, and peers, and the behaviors needed to meet those expected results. Solicitation of feedback from significant parties on progress being made in meeting their expectations will be included.

The executive coaching process will be greatly enhanced through the use of reflective learning journals completed by the leader, submitted to the coach for review, and then discussed by the leader and her coach. Coaching consists of face-to-face interactions between the coach and the leaders as well as telephone and e-mail exchanges.

CONCLUSION

Throughout my entire career, I have benefited from mentors and coaches. Mentors were of more help with a specific job, helping me to understand strategies and techniques for becoming successful. Mentors were especially helpful early in my career when I had entry and mid-level leadership roles.

I have worked with coaches, one in particular, for more than 20 years. A coach will tell you when you have started believing your own press releases or when you are neglecting your family and don't realize it, or when you enjoyed firing someone a little too much. A good coach can help you take a situation and reframe it using "a new pair of eyes" and see things that you hadn't seen before. A good coach is a critical friend and confidante.

The message is clear. You need a mentor in your life. If you are going to be "all that you can be," you will capture the opportunity for on-going development with a coach. You will also learn from serving as a mentor and a coach for others.

ENGAGING SELF AND OTHERS

The following activities and materials are designed to involve you, the reader, and others, as you and they create learning communities. Because our major emphasis in this book is on leadership lessons for adults, the exercises focus on adult learning.

Activity 13.1

Place a checkmark next to each of the following techniques/principles that you employ in your role as a leader.

- ❑ Employ a standardized procedure for determining coaching and mentoring needs.
- ❑ Use outstanding existing personnel in the organization to provide mentoring services.
- ❑ Involve personnel in both providing and receiving mentoring services.
- ❑ Ensure that the resources are available to provide coaching services for developing leaders.
- ❑ Provide training for mentors.
- ❑ Ensure that new personnel have the opportunity for mentoring and coaching as needed.
- ❑ Has criteria and procedures for evaluating coaching and mentoring efforts.
- ❑ Recognize and reward outstanding mentoring and coaching efforts.

Activity 13.2

Do you believe that the lowest-paid employee in your organization should be provided with appropriate coaching and mentoring? Provide the rationale to support your answer.

_____

_____

_____

_____

Activity 13.3

If you had a limited budget for improving the performance and skills of your employees, indicate whether you would use it for:

a) Traditional staff development
b) Coaching and mentoring
c) Both traditional staff development and coaching and mentoring—you would divide the funds between them

If you selected (c), what percent of the funds would you assign to:

Traditional training	_____ %
Coaching and mentoring	_____ %
TOTAL	100%

Activity 13.4

In regard to providing coaching/mentoring to your employees, do you believe:

1. You currently have in your organization individuals who are capable of providing mentoring/coaching services?
   ❏ Yes
   ❏ No

2. That individuals can learn by serving as a mentor/coach as well as receiving mentoring and coaching services?
   ❏ Yes
   ❏ No

3. That mentoring and coaching have the potential to make a positive impact on your organization?
   ❏ Yes
   ❏ No

In rank order (1 = highest and 4 = lowest), indicate the value you received from various types of learning experiences: [au—OK? Otherwise, what is the lowest rank order?]

Rank	Type of Learning Experience
_____	Formal college/university courses
_____	In-service staff development
_____	Coaching/mentoring
_____	Job-related activities

Activity 13.5

We would not be in the positions we presently occupy without having had the benefit of coaching or mentoring. One or more people in our lives helped us see how our talents, some of which we didn't even know we had, could be realized.

Identify some of the coaches/mentors who have helped you become the person you are as a leader in your organization, then briefly describe their contribution to your growth and development.

_____

_____

_____

_____

_____

_____

_____

Leadership Seminar Participant Responses:

> I dropped out of basketball in the seventh grade and took a job after school cleaning downtown offices. I didn't have to have the extra money, but I enjoyed having it. The new eighth-grade coach came down to one of the offices I was cleaning before the start of the basketball season and said that, with my talent, I should be on the junior high team. He was a young guy with a lot of energy, and he had played baseball for the Toledo Mud Hens. I really admired him and couldn't believe that he went out of his way to recruit me. I quit my job and played basketball through high school and college. And I ran cross country and track when I wasn't playing basketball since I didn't have a job. It is only in recent years that I realized this coach really turned my life around. I wouldn't be in sports management today if he hadn't made the effort to recruit me.

> After getting my Ph.D., I took my first university teaching position. I was one of 13 assistant professors in a doctorate-granting university where research and writing were expected and rewarded. Although I had done research and writing at the dissertation stage in doctoral study, I really didn't know if I was cut out for a career in a doctorate-granting university. For some reason, the newly appointed dean took the time to teach me "the ropes." In fact, we wrote several books together. Doing this introduced some pressure in my life given his high standards, but I can never thank him enough for helping me learn the attitudes and skills necessary to make it in a doctorate-granting university.

I was a "Lone Ranger" during the first part of my business career. I kept to myself, did good work and was promoted quickly. What I had not learned was how to be a good team member. I think that a senior co-worker recognized my problem and quietly nudged me along by offering me ad hoc assignments that required teamwork. I resisted her effort at first, but I soon discovered that going to work and doing my work was much more rewarding and even fun now that I had learned how to be a better team player.

One of the main things that it took me a few years at work to learn is that the protégé usually has to seek the mentor. Perhaps this is largely because the mentor is busy and might think it presumptuous to make advances to the beginner. At any rate, I respected a seasoned worker from day one and began to ask advice as to how to do certain things that were new to me. As a result, we struck up a good professional relationship that has been personally and professionally rewarding.

COMPLEMENTARY COMMENTARY

We have found it quite amazing how words of encouragement and seasoned advice, often small in detail, can make a positive difference in the professional life of another worker. Coaching or mentoring can certainly play a major role in the culture of the organization.

CASE 13: Receiving and Passing the Torch

Getting and passing on "the torch" that symbolizes the source of light is a common theme in the history of civilization. During the beginning stage of your career, you were probably full of idealism and energy. With time you probably learned to temper your idealism with the reality of what can go wrong as well as right, and you also learned to pace yourself with regard to the expenditure of energy. It is during the beginning stage of your career that you may begin to profit from the counsel and advocacy of a coach or mentor.

During the mid-stage of your career, and certainly during the latter stages of your career, you are sometimes asked to serve as mentor to those who are relatively recent hires. It is interesting that in most cases the protégé turns to the mentor rather than vice versa. There are times in your career when you are both mentor and protégé to different people. You are passing the torch to one person while at the same time receiving it from another.

What role or roles are you playing at this time in your career? What are the benefits and challenges you have or are receiving in this role or in these roles?

_____

_____

_____

_____

_____

_____

_____

Authors' Recommendations

Much, if not most, of the progress one makes in a career depends on one's informal networking skills. It is important that you recognize this and precisely what these networking skills are. Those who reward you for your networking ability sometimes expect qualities that contradict each other. For example, they expect loyalty, often in the form of deference, while at the same time wanting straight signals, which, when given, can make them annoyed or even angry.

Because the mentor-protégé or coach-student relationship depends on informal networking skills, the sharing of confidential information and the value of teaching-learning are essential values to a relationship of trust and respect. The protégé who is a quick study may demonstrate abilities that surpass the mentor, thus challenging the nature of the relationship of trust and respect that were previously established. As one mentor interpreted this, "Disciples always betray the master."

Alan Watts, author of the classic work titled *In My Own Way*, stated that once the student gets the message, he or she either becomes your friend or goes away. Mentors and protégés must be prepared for changes in their relationship as these changes occur in their own growth.

There is no substitute for a relationship or covenant that values an honest sharing of ideas and feelings above all. And it is important, as the relationship unfolds, that both parties to it emphasize what is conserved as well as what is changed. Respect for the growth in each person is something to be celebrated.

SELF INVENTORY

Now that you have completed the readings and activities on "The Power of Coaching and Mentoring," think about what you've learned and respond to the following items on a five-point scale: 1 (low) to 5 (high).

1. I believe that coaching/mentoring is an important part of effective leadership.   _____

2. I can identify and describe how mentors/coaches have been an important part of my leadership education.   _____

3. My enthusiasm for leadership and making a difference will stand me well as a mentor/coach.   _____

4. I gain confidence by preparing the way or doing my homework as a leader.   _____

5. Effective mentoring/coaching depends on having certain fundamentals in mind—fundamentals that keep the leader from being distracted. I am conscious of this important understanding as a leader.   _____

6. As a leader, I can be both tough and civilized.   _____

7. I can be confident without being arrogant.   _____

8. I recognize that expertise is a longer-lasting source of power than positional authority—a source of power that earns the leader respect.   _____

9. I know what to say and what not to say.   _____

10. I am able to balance my personal life with my work life.   _____

Note: If you are in a group setting, form discussion groups in order to share and summarize findings.

Scoring for Self Inventory
    Total the ratings and find your score in the following scale:

41–50	Superior
31–40	Above Average
21–30	Average
11–20	Below Average
0–10	Poor

SUGGESTED READINGS

Crow, G. J., & Matthews, J. L. (1998). *Finding One's Way: How Mentoring Can Lead to Dynamic Leadership.* Thousand Oaks, CA: Corwin Press.

Daresh, J. C. (2001). *Leaders Helping Leaders: A Practical Guide to Administrative Mentoring.* Thousand Oaks, CA: Corwin Press.

Fortgang, L. B. (1998). *Take Yourself to the Top: The Secrets of America's #1 Career Coach.* New York: Warner Books.

Lindley, F. A. (2003). *The Portable Mentor: A Resource Guide for Entry-Year Principals and Mentors.* Thousand Oaks, CA: Corwin Press.

Lombardo, M., & Eichinger, R. (2000). *For Your Improvement: A Development and Coaching Guide.* Minneapolis: Lominger Limited, Inc.

Appendix A

Behavioral Change Survey

This survey, which is a combination of 13 surveys associated with powers related to leadership, was designed to permit readers and/or participants in training associated with the book, to determine their current standing or change in behavior relative to those 13 leadership powers.

Respondents to this survey should first indicate whether they are assigning ratings to their current status in regard to employing the leadership power under consideration *or* as a measure of change in their behavior over a period of time. Following this designation, they should assign a rating to each of the power statements below by using either the current status or behavioral change descriptors and rating.

Please indicate the reason you are responding to this survey. Check **one.**		
❐ To evaluate my current behavior or status	OR	❐ To indicate change in behavior over a period of time
Status Descriptors	*Rating*	*Behavioral Change Descriptors*
Employ to a VERY GREAT degree	5	Made SIGNIFICANT POSITIVE change
Employ to a GREAT degree	4	Made SOME POSITIVE change
Employ to SOME degree	3	Made NO change
Employ to a LITTLE degree	2	Made SOME NEGATIVE change
Employ to NO degree	1	Made SIGNIFICANT NEGATIVE change

Now, assign ratings to the statements below, using *either* the status *or* behavioral change descriptors shown above.

The Power of Vision Leadership Power Statements: You . . .	Rating: *Status OR Change*
1. Anticipate that which may or will occur or come to be.	5 4 3 2 1
2. Possess a valid vision.	5 4 3 2 1
3. Are able to discern what is possible and impossible in the future.	5 4 3 2 1
4. Have the capacity to influence others to identify with your vision.	5 4 3 2 1
5. Articulate vision clearly and forcefully.	5 4 3 2 1
6. Focus on vision without being sidetracked by unimportant extraneous matters.	5 4 3 2 1
7. Stand by your convictions when criticized, ridiculed, or attacked by others.	5 4 3 2 1
8. Plan and take steps to assure that your vision becomes a reality.	5 4 3 2 1

The Power of Identifying and Using Your Talents Leadership Power Statements: You . . .	Rating: *Status OR Change*
1. Use various methods to identify talents.	5 4 3 2 1
2. Are able to identify your own strengths and weaknesses.	5 4 3 2 1
3. Use knowledge of your own and others' strengths and weaknesses in assuming or delegating jobs and responsibilities.	5 4 3 2 1
4. Match job requirements with skills and abilities.	5 4 3 2 1
5. Set personal goals that are consistent with talents, but at the same time are challenging.	5 4 3 2 1
6. Accentuate positive talents while eliminating the negative (weaknesses).	5 4 3 2 1
7. Recognize and use the varying talents of people in building teams.	5 4 3 2 1
8. Are able to identify and learn from those who have special talents.	5 4 3 2 1

The Power of Learning Leadership Power Statements: You . . .	*Rating:* *Status OR Change*				
1. Realize that learning is a major tool in developing leadership traits.	5	4	3	2	1
2. Understand that one can improve his or her leadership skills by reflecting upon and learning from past experiences.	5	4	3	2	1
3. Appreciate that frequently people learn more from failures than successes.	5	4	3	2	1
4. Accept the fact that the most meaningful learning takes place through doing and experiencing	5	4	3	2	1
5. Realize that you have to relearn and adjust because of the rapid changes in technology and society.	5	4	3	2	1
6. Understand that meaningful learning can take place through the association and observations of others.	5	4	3	2	1
7. Refute the notion that you can't "teach old dogs new tricks."	5	4	3	2	1
8. Realize that learning and knowledge open many opportunities to lead and serve others.	5	4	3	2	1

The Power of Competence Leadership Power Statements: You . . .	*Rating:* *Status OR Change*				
1. Understand the relationship between being competent and being a competent leader.	5	4	3	2	1
2. Are capable of identifying and using competencies of others.	5	4	3	2	1
3. Are able to identify and benefit from own weaknesses and strengths.	5	4	3	2	1
4. Delegate certain tasks and responsibilities to those who are more competent.	5	4	3	2	1
5. Provide training and other opportunities for people to become more competent.	5	4	3	2	1
6. Set goals and develop a plan for becoming more competent.	5	4	3	2	1
7. Give credit to those who utilize their competencies for helping others.	5	4	3	2	1
8. Use skills and abilities for the betterment of mankind.	5	4	3	2	1

The Power of Wanting to Be There Leadership Power Statements: You . . .	Rating: Status OR Change
1. Understand the importance of showing others that you wish to serve in your current role.	5 4 3 2 1
2. Demonstrate that you are confident that you can fulfill the responsibilities of a position.	5 4 3 2 1
3. Make associates and subordinates feel comfortable in relating to and following you.	5 4 3 2 1
4. Interact with followers and others in a friendly and productive manner.	5 4 3 2 1
5. Demonstrate that you support wholeheartedly the mission and goals of your organization.	5 4 3 2 1
6. Are proud of the organization's mission and goals.	5 4 3 2 1
7. Demonstrate to associates and subordinates that you are concerned about their welfare.	5 4 3 2 1
8. Demonstrate that you will not "abandon the ship" when things get rough.	5 4 3 2 1

The Power of Passion Leadership Power Statements: You . . .	Rating: Status OR Change
1. Realize the role that passion plays in leading and influencing.	5 4 3 2 1
2. Are skillful in determining when and how to use passion when leading.	5 4 3 2 1
3. Strive to get followers to use passion in appropriate ways.	5 4 3 2 1
4. Use emotion and feeling in promoting and defending the cause of the organization.	5 4 3 2 1
5. Are adept in using symbolism, folktales, personal references, and so forth in support of the organization's mission.	5 4 3 2 1
6. Give your heart and soul in support of your beliefs and convictions.	5 4 3 2 1
7. Are adept at using failures, disaster, mishaps, and the like to rally people to work for a worthy cause.	5 4 3 2 1
8. Encourage self and others to adopt the attitude and belief that nothing is impossible when you tackle a task with enthusiasm and passion.	5 4 3 2 1

The Power of Hope Leadership Power Statements: You . . .	Rating: Status OR Change				
1. Realize the importance of the power of hope in striving to lead and reach goals.	5	4	3	2	1
2. Have trust that conscientious people will attain goals regardless of the roadblocks.	5	4	3	2	1
3. Make things "hoped for" become reality through planning, leading, and directing.	5	4	3	2	1
4. Have trust that workers and all stakeholders believe that goals will be attained.	5	4	3	2	1
5. Take care not to hope for things that are impossible or improbable.	5	4	3	2	1
6. Are skillful in incorporating hope and trust with the vision of better things in the future.	5	4	3	2	1
7. Reflect and benefit from examples of how leaders in the past used hope to assist them in realizing impossible dreams.	5	4	3	2	1
8. Realize that without hope there is little chance that desired outcomes will be realized.	5	4	3	2	1

The Power of Keeping the fire Leadership Power Statements: You . . .	Rating: Status OR Change				
1. Realize that enthusiasm is contagious and few victories can be realized without it.	5	4	3	2	1
2. Strive to encourage others and self to be "upbeat" in carrying out responsibilities.	5	4	3	2	1
3. Use strategies to renew and maintain enthusiasm when work becomes routine and dull.	5	4	3	2	1
4. Are careful to be sincere and straightforward in displaying enthusiasm for the cause of the organization.	5	4	3	2	1
5. Strive to develop a culture in the organization that is characterized by a "gung–ho" attitude.	5	4	3	2	1
6. Respect and promote individuals who sincerely demonstrate enthusiasm for their work.	5	4	3	2	1
7. Emphasize "walking the walk" or follow through more than "talking the talk" or just voicing enthusiasm.	5	4	3	2	1
8. Give attention to "keeping the fire alive" among workers who tend to lose their enthusiasm.	5	4	3	2	1

The Power of Determination Leadership Power Statements: You . . .	Rating: Status OR Change
1. Realize the power of determination in leading and reaching goals.	5 4 3 2 1
2. Exercise good judgment concerning when to continue fighting and when to "throw in the towel."	5 4 3 2 1
3. Adopt a personal philosophy that ensures that "when the going gets tough, the tough get going."	5 4 3 2 1
4. Understand that self-discipline and commitment to hard work, rather than sentimentality, bring success.	5 4 3 2 1
5. Do not let defeat or setbacks deter the quest to meet established or desired goals.	5 4 3 2 1
6. Set examples of resolve that can be emulated by others.	5 4 3 2 1
7. Reflect on past examples of personal use of determination to overcome difficulties in order to strengthen resolve to do better in the future.	5 4 3 2 1
8. Surround yourself with colleagues, team members, and others who are endowed with confidence.	5 4 3 2 1

The Power of Gratitude Leadership Power Statements: You . . .	Rating: Status OR Change
1. Appreciate the importance of the power of gratitude in leading and managing.	5 4 3 2 1
2. Show gratitude to all those who support and work for the cause.	5 4 3 2 1
3. Recognize and celebrate the successes and good fortune of others.	5 4 3 2 1
4. Use simple but thoughtful means (i.e., notes) to express gratitude to those who do well or contribute.	5 4 3 2 1
5. Give credit to those who have preceded you in a job.	5 4 3 2 1
6. Give colleagues and subordinates credit for organizational successes.	5 4 3 2 1
7. Show gratitude to those who give you honest feedback and point out personal weaknesses.	5 4 3 2 1
8. Are thankful and grateful for the opportunity to contribute and serve.	5 4 3 2 1

The Power of Private Victories *Leadership Power Statements: You . . .*	*Rating:* *Status OR Change*
1. Realize the importance of the power of private victories in leading and managing.	5 4 3 2 1
2. Are able to draw pleasure and strength from overcoming bad personal habits or behavior.	5 4 3 2 1
3. Relate to colleagues and others the power that one can gain by reflecting upon but not bragging about personal victories.	5 4 3 2 1
4. Recognize that seemingly small behaviors are the mortar that holds the most dramatic bricks of an organization in place.	5 4 3 2 1
5. Learn to determine own worth through reflecting on private victories rather than depending on others to tell you who you are.	5 4 3 2 1
6. Understand that one of the most rewarding private victories of life is becoming an independent, responsible individual.	5 4 3 2 1
7. Refrain from boasting about successes.	5 4 3 2 1
8. Give credit to self for jobs well done.	5 4 3 2 1

The Power of Your Moral Compass *Leadership Power Statements: You . . .*	*Rating:* *Status OR Change*
1. Realize the power of a moral compass in leading and managing.	5 4 3 2 1
2. Understand that the behavior of leaders, whether good or bad, sets examples for followers.	5 4 3 2 1
3. Strive to create an organizational culture that encourages employees to be honorable and decent.	5 4 3 2 1
4. Make decisions and take actions that are in the best interest of you and your organization.	5 4 3 2 1
5. Develop a set of core values and beliefs for staff and self.	5 4 3 2 1
6. Become involved in spiritual activities.	5 4 3 2 1
7. Provide training that emphasizes ethical standards.	5 4 3 2 1
8. Set example for others through his or her own exemplary behavior.	5 4 3 2 1

The Power of Coaching and Mentoring Leadership Power Statements: You . . .	Rating: Status OR Change
1. Realize that power that can be derived from coaching/mentoring.	5 4 3 2 1
2. Establish procedures so that coaching/mentoring is a regular part of the organization's training/improvement program.	5 4 3 2 1
3. Take advantage of using outstanding leaders/managers for personal improvement efforts.	5 4 3 2 1
4. Identify and use leaders in own organization to serve as mentors and coaches.	5 4 3 2 1
5. Use networking to identify leaders who can provide coaching/mentoring services.	5 4 3 2 1
6. Conduct needs assessment to identify leadership/management areas that need improvement.	5 4 3 2 1
7. Develop and maintain a program that provides support (buddy system) for new employees.	5 4 3 2 1
8. Sets up incentive programs to reward and recognize outstanding coaches and methods.	5 4 3 2 1

Scoring and Interpretation

Individual item scores (104) and 13 different leadership power scores are obtained through administering this survey instrument. The item score is simply the rating (between 1 and 5) that was assigned by the participant. Each of the 13 power scores is obtained by adding the 8 item ratings in each particular power. The range in total scores for each power is from eight (8) and forty (40).

The interpretation procedures for the 13 power categories for both the CURRENT STATUS and BEHAVIORAL CHANGE administrations follow:

Total Score Interpretation

Status Interpretation	Rating	Behavioral Change Interpretation
Employ to a VERY GREAT degree	32 and above	Made SIGNIFICANT POSITIVE change
Employ to a GREAT degree	26–31	Made SOME POSITIVE change
Employ to SOME degree	20–25	Made NO change
Employ to a LITTLE degree	14–19	Made SOME NEGATIVE change
Employ to NO degree	8–13	Made SIGNIFICANT NEGATIVE change

A form for recording and presenting the 13 power categories is shown on the next page.

FORM FOR RECORDING AND PRESENTING
LEADERSHIP CATEGORY POWER SCORES

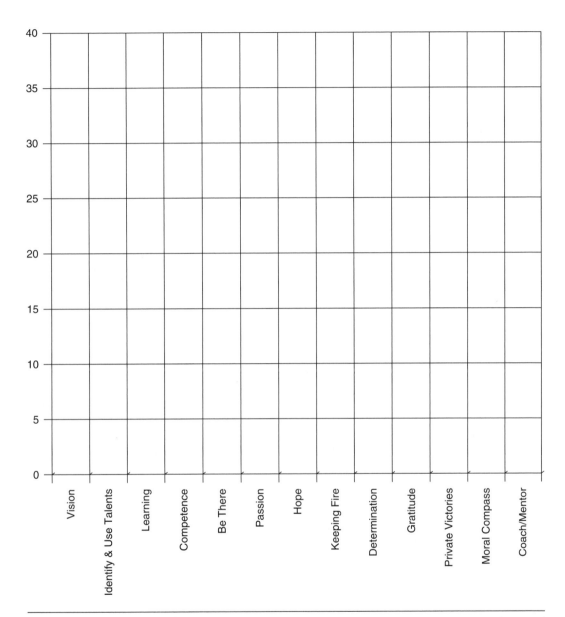

Notes

INTRODUCTION

1. Rollo May, *Power and Innocence* (New York: Norton & Co., 1972), p. 50.
2. Ibid.
3. Hedrick Smith, *The Power Game* (New York: Random House, 1988), p. xxii.
4. Morgan W. McCall, Jr., *High Fliers: Developing the Next Generation of Leaders* (Boston: Harvard Business School Press, 1988), p. 189.
5. Ibid., p. 157.
6. Ibid., p. 189.
7. Arnold A. Hutschnecker, *The Drive for Power* (New York: Evans and Co., 1974), p. 8.
8. McCall, *High Fliers*, p. 136.
9. Ibid., p. 156.

CHAPTER 1

1. *Time*, May 18, 1987, p. 68.
2. William F. Buckley, Jr., *Atlantic High* (Boston: Little, Brown, 1982), p. 239.
3. Quoted in Burt Nanus. *Visionary Leadership—Creating a Compelling Sense of Direction for Your Organization* (San Francisco: Jossey-Bass Publishers, 1992).

CHAPTER 3

1. Gloria Steinem, *Revolution From Within: A Book of Self-Esteem* (Boston: Little, Brown, 1992), p. 68.

CHAPTER 6

1. Andy Dougan, *Robin Williams* (New York: Thunder's Mouth Press, 1998), p. 154.
2. Arthur M. Schlesinger Jr., *A Life in the Twentieth Century* (Boston: Houghton Mifflin, 2000), p. 282.

CHAPTER 8

1. William F. Buckley, Jr., *Airborne* (Boston: Little, Brown, 1976).
2. Dale L. Brubaker, "The Power in Keeping the Fire," *Business Life*, Sept. 2000, p. 41.

CHAPTER 13

1. Morley Fraser, Letter to the senior author. February 21, 1989.
2. Ibid.
3. *New York Times*, September 30, 1988, p. 22.
4. Peter Hart, *New York Times*, May 30, 1988, p. 11.
5. Quoted in ibid.
6. Paul Gigot, *The Wall Street Journal*, September 30, 1988, p. 22.
7. Morley Fraser, Letter to the senior author. February 21, 1989.
8. *Washington Post*, November 12, 1988, p. 1.

References

Adams, J. (1983). *Without Precedent*. New York: Putnam.

Anderson, T. (1994). *Den of Lions*. New York: Mass Market Paperback.

Brubaker, D. L. (1994). *Creative Curriculum Leadership*. Thousand Oaks, CA: Corwin Press.

Brubaker, D. L. (2000, August). "The Power in Keeping the Fire." *Business Life*, 40–41.

Brubaker, D. L., & Coble, L. D. (1997). *Staying on Track: An Educational Leader's Guide to Preventing Derailment and Ensuring Personal and Organizational Success*. Thousand Oaks, CA: Corwin Press.

Buckley, W. F., Jr. (1976). *Airborne*. Boston: Little, Brown.

Buckley, W. F., Jr. (1983). *Atlantic High*. Boston: Little, Brown.

Dougan, A., & Williams, R. (1999). *Robin Williams: A Biography*. New York: Thunder's Mouth.

Gardner, H. (1983). *Frames of Mind: The Theory of Multiple Intelligences*. New York: Basic Books.

Goffman, E. (1959). *The Presentation of Self in Everyday Life*. New York: Doubleday Anchor.

Graham, K. (1997). *Personal History*. New York: Vintage Books.

Halberstam, D. (2001). *War in a Time of Peace*. New York: Random House.

Hemingway, E. (1929). *A Farewell to Arms*. New York: Simon & Schuster.

Hutschnecker, A. (1974). *The Drive for Power*. New York: Evans.

Josephson, M. (1990). *Making Ethical Decisions*. Marina Del Rey, CA: The Josephson Institute of Ethics.

Kinard, L. (1997). *Good Morning*. Winston-Salem, NC: Down Home Press.

Kleinfeld, S. (1989). *The Hotel*. New York: Simon & Schuster.

Levinson, D. et al. (1978). *The Seasons of a Man's Life*. New York: Random House.

Levinson, D. et al. (1997). *The Seasons of a Woman's Life*. New York: Random House.

Linver, S. (1978). *Speakeasy*. New York: Summit.

May, R. (1972). *Power and Innocence*. New York: Norton.

McCall, M. W., Jr. (1988). *High Fliers: Developing the Next Generation of Leaders*. Boston: Harvard Business School Press.

McCall, M. W., Jr., Lombardo, M., & Morrison, A. (1988). *The Lessons of Experience*. Lexington, MA: Lexington Books.

Nanus, B. (1992). *Visionary Leadership—Creating a Compelling Sense of Direction for Your Organization*. San Francisco: Jossey-Bass.

Putnam, R. D. (2000). *Bowling Alone: The Collapse and Revival of American Community*. New York: Simon & Schuster.

Schlesinger, A. M., Jr. (2000). *A Life in the 20th Century*. New York: Houghton Mifflin.

Senge, P. (1990). *The Fifth Discipline.* New York: Doubleday.

Smith, H. (1988). *The Power Game.* New York: Random House.

Steinem, G. (1992). *Revolution From Within.* Boston: Little, Brown.

Vygotsky, L. S. (1978). *Mind in Society: The Development of Higher Psychological Processes.* Cambridge, MA: Harvard University Press.

Watts, A. (1972). *In My Own Way.* New York: Pantheon Books.

Index

A
Activities
  behavioral change survey, 205–213
  coaching and mentoring, 197–202
  competence, 63–73
  contradictions, 33–37
  determination, 140–145
  gratitude, 152–158
  hope, 108–114
  keeping the fire, 121–133
  learning experiences, 45–53
  moral compass, 183–189
  motivation and
    wanting to be there, 80–88
  passion, 93–99
  private victory, 164–171
  self-inventory, 19–20
  team-building, 28–37
  visioning, 10–19
Adams, J., 69
Albright, Madeline, 4
Ambition, 62
American Red Cross, 76
Anderson, Terry, 40
Articulating a vision, 4–5
Atlantic High, 5
Austin, Gerald, 22–23

B
Barton, Clara, 76
Behavioral change survey, 205–213
Big-picture skills, 61–62
Bolman, Lee, 106
Bonaparte, Napoleon, 105
Buckley, William F., 5
Bush, George H. W., 76, 191, 192

C
Carter, Jimmy, 4
Center for Creative Leadership, 116
Chief Learning Officers (CLOs), 50–52

Childhood experiences reflection, 8
Churchill, Winston, 69
Civic duty, 180
Clinton, Bill, 4
Coaching and mentoring
  activities, 197–202
  behavioral change survey, 212
  benefits for leaders, 193–194
  model for, 195–196
  necessity of, 194–195
  power of, 195
  self inventory, 202
Coldwater Corporation, The, 191–193
Collaboration and collegiality, 150
Commitment Scale, 116–117
Communication
  of visions, 9
  public speaking and, 68–70
  written, 70–71
Competence
  activities, 63–73
  behavioral change survey, 207
  identifying incompetence and, 56–57
  importance of
    feedback in building, 58–59
  leadership and, 57–58
  perceptions of others and, 61–63
  self inventory, 73
  versus incompetence, 56–57, 59–60
Concern for others, 179
Connection, sense of, 148
Control and determination, 138–139

D
Deal, Terrence, 106
Den of Lions, 40
Determination
  activities, 140–145
  behavioral change survey, 210
  benefits of leaders', 137
  control and, 138–139

self inventory, 144–145
what creates, 136–137
work ethic, 138
Disney, Walt, 6–7
Dole, Elizabeth, 76
DuVall, Lloyd, 135–137

E
Empathizing, 106–107
Empowerment in
    team-building, 26–28
Entrance and exit rituals, 65–66
Expansive personalities, 118–119,
    122–126
Experience, learning from, 42–44

F
Fairness, 178–179
Farewell to Arms, A, 40
Fifth Discipline, The, 169
Follow up and follow through, 61
Followership, 107
Fortgang, Laura Berman, 193
Fraser, Morley, 191–192

G
Galbraith, Ken, 5
Garrett, Norman, III, 159–161
Gerber, Robin, 104
Gigot, Paul, 192
Goffman, Erving, 19, 173
Gonzalez-Balado, Jose Luis, 175
Good Morning Show, The, 3
Graham, Katharine, 91
Gratitude
    activities, 152–158
    and learning what not to do, 151
    behavioral change survey, 210
    collaboration and collegiality
        with, 150
    formal approaches for
        expressing, 150–151
    power of persuasion
        and, 149–150
    self inventory, 157–158
    sense of connection and, 148
    the personal touch and, 150

H
Halberstam, David, 3, 136
Hart, Peter, 192
Hemingway, Ernest, 40
Hesburgh, Theodore Martin, 4

Honesty, 176–177
Hope
    behavioral change survey, 209
    empathy and, 106–107
    examples of, 103–105
    followership and, 107
    organizational change
        and, 107–108
    self inventory, 113–114
Hotel, The, 65

I
Incompetence versus competence,
    56–57, 59–60
Integrity, 177

J
Josephson, Michael, 176

K
Keeping the fire
    activities, 121–133
    behavioral change survey, 209
    expansive personality and,
        118–119, 122–126
    finding and, 116–117
    making inner shifts for, 119–120
    self inventory, 132–133
Kennedy, John F., 90
Kinard, Lee, 3–4
King, Martin Luther, Jr., 104
Kleinfield, S., 65

L
Law abidingness, 180
Leadership
    and relationships with
        others, 78–79
    as gift giving, 106–107
    behavioral change survey, 205–213
    coaching, mentoring, and, 193–196
    competency and, 56–63
    determination and, 137–139
    genetic predisposition and early
        developmental experiences in, 92
    gratitude and, 149–152
    hope and, 105–108
    identifying talents for, 23–24
    keeping the fire, 117–120
    learning new skills for, 41–45
    moral compass for, 175–182
    motivation and wanting
        to be there, 77–80

passion and, 91–93
private victories and, 161–164
shaping process in, 23–24
table manners of, 71–72
types, 125–126
visionary, 5–9
wanting to be there
    versus upward mobility, 78
*Leadership in the Eleanor
    Roosevelt Way,* 104
Leading With Soul, 106
Learning
    activities, 45–53
    and competence building, 59
    behavioral change survey, 207
    from experience, 42–44
    new skills for leadership, 39–40
    principles and procedures
        involved in successful, 44–45
    reflective learning journals for, 41–42
    self-inventory, 52–53
    styles, recognizing different, 21–22
Lennon, John, 115
Lessons of Experience, The, 112
Levinson, Daniel, 132
Life balance, 80
Listening skills, 67
Lombardo, Michael, 112
Loyalty, 178
Lynch, Dotty, 192

M
Making Ethical Decisions, 176
Mazda Miata Club of America, 159–162
McCall, Morgan, 112
Moral compass
    activities, 183–189
    behavioral change survey, 211
    concern for others and, 179
    cultural components and, 176
    fairness and, 178–179
    honesty and, 176–177
    in rough times, 173–175
    integrity and, 177
    law abidingness/civic duty and, 180
    loyalty and, 178
    personal accountability and, 181
    promise keeping and, 177–178
    pursuit of excellence and, 180–181
    respect for others and, 179–180
    self inventory, 189
    spirituality and, 181–182
Morrison, Ann, 112

Mother Teresa, 175
Mother Teresa: In My Own Words, 175
Motivation and wanting to be there
    activities, 80–88
    behavioral change survey, 208
    changing organizational
        culture to improve, 79–80
    finding, 76–77
    importance of leaders', 75–76
    life balance and, 80
    reasons for, 77–79
    self inventory, 88
Murrow, Edward R., 76
My American Journey, 3

N
National Football League, 22–23
Nelson, Roland, 116
New York Times, 192
Nixon, Richard, 76

O
O'Connor, Carroll, 90

P
Pain and passion, 92
Passion
    activities, 93–99
    behavioral change survey, 208
    benefits of leaders', 90–91
    creating ones', 90
    genetic predisposition and
        early developmental
        experiences and, 92
    pain and, 92
    personal and organization
        success and, 93
    personnel and, 93
    self inventory, 98–99
Perfectionist-systematizers, 126
Personal accountability, 181
Personal History, 91
Personal touch, the, 150
Personnel and passion, 93
Persuasion, power of, 149–150
Player, Gary, 117
Powell, Colin, 3, 4
Power Game, The, 192
*Presentation of Self
    In Everyday Life, The,* 19, 173
Private victories
    activities, 164–171
    behavioral change survey, 211

celebrating, 163–164
defined, 162
meaning of, 160–161
self inventory, 171
taking charge of, 162–163
Procrastination, 62–63
Promise keeping, 177–178
Public speaking, 68–70
Pursuit of excellence, 180–181

R
Reagan, Ronald, 76, 192
Reflective learning journals, 41–42
Respect for others, 179–180
Revolution From Within, 40
Road and Track, 160
Roosevelt, Eleanor, 104

S
Schlesinger, Arthur M., Jr., 90–91, 96
Scowcroft, Brent, 136
Seasons of a Man's Life, The, 132
Seasons of a Woman's Life, The, 132
Self inventories
    coaching and mentoring, 202
    competence, 73
    determination, 144–145
    gratitude, 157–158
    hope, 113–114
    keeping the fire, 132–133
    learning, 52–53
    moral compass, 189
    motivation and wanting
        to be there, 88
    passion, 98–99
    private victory, 171
    talent identification, 37
    vision, 19–20
Self-vindicators/fix-it specialists, 126
Senge, P., 169
Smith, Hedrick, 192
Spiritual journey and
    leadership, 181–182
*Staying on Track:
    An Educational Leaders' Guide to
    Preventing Derailment...*, 65

Steinem, Gloria, 40
Striver-Builder leaders, 125–126

T
Table manners of leadership, 71–72
*Take Yourself to the Top: The Secrets
    of America's #1 Career Coach*, 193
Talents and team-building
    activities, 28–37
    behavioral change survey, 206
    empowerment during, 26–28
    identifying individual, 22–23
    self-inventory, 37
    work groups versus teams in, 24–26
Teeter, Robert, 191–193
Television speaking, 69–70
Transformational visioning, 6–8

U
Uhlig, George, 89–90
United States Sports Academy, 89–90

V
Vision
    activities on formulating, 10–20
    articulating, 4–5
    as a source of power, 3–4
    behavioral change survey, 206
    childhood experiences shaping, 8
    communicating, 9
    implementing, 17–19
    of Walt Disney, 6–7
    personal, 7–8
    process of visioning in realizing, 5–6
    self inventory, 19–20
    transformational visioning in
        realizing, 6–8

W
War in a Time of Peace, 3, 136
Washington Post, 91, 192
Williams, Robin, 90
Without Precedent, 69
Work ethic, 138
Work groups versus teams, 24–26
Written communications, 70–71

**CORWIN
PRESS**

The Corwin Press logo—a raven striding across an open book—represents the union of courage and learning. Corwin Press is committed to improving education for all learners by publishing books and other professional development resources for those serving the field of K–12 education. By providing practical, hands-on materials, Corwin Press continues to carry out the promise of its motto: **"Helping Educators Do Their Work Better."**